CRACKING UP

*My 25 years of writing,
performing, and producing
comedy in Hollywood*

Ed Driscoll

Cracking Up

My 25 years of writing, performing, and producing comedy in Hollywood

Ed Driscoll

ISBN (Print Edition): 979-8-35097-136-1

ISBN (eBook Edition): 979-8-35097-137-8

This book shares the personal experiences of the author. In some instances, he has changed names and circumstances to protect the privacy of his friends, family, and colleagues.

FOR DMD

INTRODUCTION

This book chronicles my twenty-five plus years in Hollywood of writing, performing, producing, and complaining. Here's what I can tell you for certain: the entertainment industry is truly a roller coaster. Which means, sometimes you laugh, sometimes you scream, and a lot of the time, you feel like you're gonna barf.

As with any roller coaster, you have that slow, nerve-wracking climb to the top, and the feeling of anticipation as you get further from the ground. Then, you're at the top, and the view is exhilarating. But it seems like you're only there for a few seconds, and the inevitable downward descent can be extremely fast and frightening. Then, there's a leveling off, followed by another climb up, followed by another plunge, and the pattern continues.

As I tell you about some of my personal experiences along this wild, weird journey, it's my hope that you'll not only be entertained, but that you'll find some of the life lessons I've learned along the way to be useful to you, as well. At the very least, as examples of what *not* to do!

I'd also like to note that some of my many crazy show-biz related stories were previously told in my first book, *Spilled Gravy*. I won't be repeating any of those stories in this book because it would be pointless, and most importantly, because I'd like you to buy *Spilled Gravy*, as well. In fact, I'll wait a moment while you order it now. (And please don't buy just one copy, then lend it to everyone you know, like my relatives did. A guy's gotta eat, right?)

Book ordered? Great, thanks, I appreciate it! And now, with all that out of the way, let's dig in, shall we?

CHAPTER 1
Awards, Rewards, & A Variety of Variety Shows

*D*ennis Miller Live on HBO was my first full-time television writing job. Well, as "full-time" as any TV writing job can be. After all, if/when the show is cancelled, you're not "full-time" anymore. Anyway, as far as jobs go, it was awesome. I'm sure I bitched and moaned about stuff while I was working there (in fact, that's actually part of the job of a comedy writer, to bitch and moan about stuff.) But I look back with great fondness on the whole experience.

How lucky I was to be in an office every day with a handful of the smartest, funniest people I'd ever met. The very first staff that Dennis assembled was an amazing group. We got our work done, which of course was the priority — most of the time — but the daily give and take amongst a bunch of cynical scribes was its own subset of entertaining ridiculousness. (Neil Simon famously wrote a play based on his experiences in the writers room of Sid Caesar's *Your Show Of Shows* called *Laughter on the 42nd Floor*.)

While most comedy writers and performers have a reputation for being self-indulgent, what's often overlooked is the fact that most of us are self-deprecating, too. Sometimes, to a fault. Personally, while I love mocking everyone, I really enjoy mocking myself even more. And part of that mockery involves making fun of whatever project or show I'm working on, even if the project is actually very good. In fact, the better something is, the more deprecating I am about it. When something is terrible, it's not as fun to ridicule it. It just seems like piling on.

"DML" as the hip people called it, (and I called it that as well,) was a critical and popular hit almost from the get-go. Which naturally resulted in all of us on staff constantly making fun of our own show. We didn't do it much in front of Dennis because after all, it was *his* show, and it would seem like we were making fun of him, which we weren't (at least, no more than he made fun of us.) While being self-deprecating can be an endearing trait, it also can come back to bite one in the ass. I've got plenty of posterior wounds to prove it.

One of the most popular features on Dennis's show was *The Big Screen*, where a news photo would emerge on-screen, and Dennis would verbally "caption" the picture. In 1994, the whole world was immersed in the O.J. Simpson trial, so we'd have lots of photos in that realm that we'd write jokes about. I remember one that I wrote, that showed O.J. over-dramatically struggling to get the famous "black gloves" on over his hands, and smirking at the jury while doing so. As the photo was displayed, Dennis, as O.J., said, "See? This doesn't fit. These are *definitely* not the gloves I wore when I killed those people." A dark joke, but funny, which was the overall theme of our show.

Our task as staff writers was to be given approximately thirty to forty wire service photos every day, and we'd have to "caption" them, that is, say something funny about what is going on in the picture, whether it's someone in the photo supposedly talking to someone else in the photo, or a song that is apropos, or simply Dennis making a funny comment. You'd try to write as many as you could, but sometimes there was a photo that just didn't inspire you, so you'd skip it. And sometimes, you'd throw in stuff that you knew wouldn't or couldn't be used on air, just to make the other writers laugh. We'd all work on the batches on our own in our individual offices, then would gather at an appointed time around a conference table. Dennis didn't sit in on these sessions. The purpose was for us all to sift through what we had, and send what was deemed worthy down to the stage, for Dennis to review during run-through.

3

As Executive Producer, Jeff Cesario would run the photo-pitch meetings, and they were always pretty fun. He'd hold up a photo, we'd go around the room and each read aloud the joke we'd written for that picture. We'd decide as a group what joke or jokes we liked best, then that photo would be sent down to the stage, along with the line or lines that accompanied it. It was always entertaining to hear what everyone had come up with. Sometimes two or more of us would have written essentially the same joke, so we'd take the best version and use that. And sometimes there was a photo where nobody really had anything great for it, so that photo would not even be loaded into the rehearsal slides.

One day, we had a random photo of a man staring angrily at his wristwatch. As purely a joke for the room, I pitched an annoyed voice saying "What the hell? How long is this show??" We all laughed, as it was just making fun of our own show, but obviously not something to be aired. We went around the table, and nobody really had anything good for the photo, so we naturally assumed that the Production Assistant in charge of bringing the jokes to the stage knew to leave that photo out.

Later that day, we were in the studio for rehearsal. When it came time to sort through *Big Screen* bits, the director would put the photos up on the screen, then Dennis would read aloud the joke or two that we'd come up with, then either laugh and say "Okay," which meant it had passed the first stage for being on the live show. Or he'd simply say "No" or "Nope," and it was out. Sometimes Dennis would say "nah" in a mumbled way, and it sounded a lot like "map." This is why the late, great Kevin Rooney dubbed these "map sessions." Kevin would mimic Dennis saying "Map, map, map, yes, map..."

We were plodding along through the process when suddenly the picture of the angry watch-staring guy popped up. I thought, huh, that's odd. I don't remember anyone having a joke for that, but I guess I missed it. I was curious to hear what it was. Dennis looked into the teleprompter and recited "What the hell? How long is this show??" We all sat frozen in horror. Somehow, the

4

Production Assistant thought we'd meant to include that "joke," so there it was. It was priceless to see Dennis's face as he tried to comprehend what the line even meant. As the realization it was an insult of our own show came to him, a confused scowl crossed his face, and he looked accusingly at the writers. We all sat there expressionless, then he shook his head in bafflement, and said, "Noooooooo!" And on we went to the next photo. From then on, I was always *extra clear* with the Production Assistants when a joke was not meant to go to the stage!

* * * *

A source of reliable amusement behind the scenes of the show was when people would get confused by Dennis's Pittsburgh accent. His was much more pronounced than mine, but as a fellow yinzer, I understood "Pittsburghese." For instance, words like "fire" and "hire" sometimes come out sounding like "fahr" and "hahr," and words like "file" and "rile" sound like "fahwl" and "rahwl." At one point, we were working on a joke that happened to be about Vanna White, and a Writers Assistant was taking dictation from all of us and typing it into a computer, which showed the document on a large monitor so that we could all see the process. Dennis came out with the line, "Hey Vanna, back off. You turn tiles for a living." But the assistant was typing it as he heard it from Dennis and his accent, and the line kept showing up on the monitor as, "You turn *towels* for a living." A puzzled, frustrated Dennis kept saying, "No, no, not 'towels.' *Towels!!*" After much guffawing by the rest of us, I was able to translate, and the line showed up correctly, eventually.

* * * *

It's always cool working at CBS Television City. So many classic shows have been shot there, *All in the Family, The Carol Burnett Show, Wheel of Fortune, The Price is Right.* Back in 1994, Vanna White was really becoming popular, as America's sweetheart. (At long last, usurping me for the title.) Everyone had a crush on Vanna, and subsequently, since she worked on that lot, there was an entire wall in the security entrance filled with nothing but pictures of her stalkers. The idea of course was that the guards double-checked to make sure that none of these folks gained access to the lot where she worked.

One day, me and one of the other writers, Greg, thought it might be amusing to gather pictures of some of our fellow writers and stick them up on the "stalker wall." So, we printed out some pics, and went down to the security lobby, and while Greg distracted the guard, I taped up the pictures of our colleagues. And we left, laughing at the thought of people seeing them up there, but honestly, we kind of forgot about it within hours as we went about our day. All in all, it was funny, that is, until the next morning when security and the police showed up at Dennis' office. Then of course, it was *really* funny.

The guard said, "Mr. Miller, we have two guys at the gate who claim they're your writers, but they're on the list as stalkers of Vanna White." For some reason, Dennis immediately turned to me.

"Do you know anything about this, Drisc?" I looked at him wide-eyed. "Um, just as much as you know," I gagged out nervously. An awkward silence ensued, and by this point, the cop was losing his patience. "Mr. Miller, we have a lot to do here today, so we just need to know, are the two guys we're holding at the front gate your writers, or are they stalkers?"

"Can't they be both?" Dennis deadpanned.

Suddenly, yet another guard entered the offices, with the two unfortunate writers who'd been trying to get into their place of work in tow. The guard asked, "Are these guys your writers?" Dennis shot me and Greg an annoyed look, then turned to the guard. After a beat or two, he said, "I've never seen them before in my life."

At that point, everyone, including the guards, burst into laughter, and they released the harried scribes into our custody. I was relieved, but as I headed back to my office, Dennis stopped me and said, "Drisc, I'm not accusing you, and that was hilarious, but don't do that again. This is a place of fucking business!" I resisted the urge to make a joke like, " 'Fucking business'? Is this a whore house?" and instead simply gave him a thumbs up and got out of there.

*   *   *   *

In truth, the writers on the show, and more specifically, me and my cohort Greg, did lots of things that would probably have gotten us fired, if not arrested, at most other jobs. (Especially these days.) But all the ridiculously immature things we did were always in good fun, never meaning to offend or embarrass anyone. Yet, we'd almost inevitably end up embarrassing ourselves in some fashion. For instance, there was a kitchen in the writers' offices, and we'd all keep our lunches and snacks and various condiments in the fridge. There was an ongoing contest to post ridiculous things on the fridge, with all sorts of stupid notes and drawings covering the fridge door as if it belonged to the parents of a truly disturbed child. One day Greg and I decided it would be good to take a few pictures of ourselves pretending to pee (or worse) into the milk and ketchup and so forth. We didn't actually photograph our genitalia, you just saw our faces and our pants unbuckled, straddling the food. (Sort of like soft porn, or so I've heard.) Then we posted those photos on the fridge itself, with the intention of leaving them up only for the afternoon until everyone had seen them. It was a Friday, which was the day we'd do our live show, so it was always a bit hectic.

As I mentioned, the *Big Screen* was a very popular segment on the show. I can't tell you how many people would call or stop me on the studio lot and say, "Hey, loved the pictures this week." Which of course I always appreciated. So I wasn't surprised on Monday morning when I was entering our offices very early, still half asleep, and a friendly female security guard walked past and said "Good morning! Hey, I really liked your pictures!" I smiled and thanked her, but I did think the smirk she displayed was a little odd. As I walked into the kitchen, I realized with horror that we'd never taken down our little photos of us with our pants down, huddled over the condiments. *Those* were the pictures she was talking about, not *The Big Screen*. I swear every time I saw her after that on the studio lot, she'd laugh and say "Hi, fridge-man!" Somewhat humiliating, but at least it seemed to make her happy.

*   *   *   *

Often our workday played out like an episode of *Larry Sanders*. That brilliant show was just a bit too close to reality for those of us ensconced in that world. The things that happened daily would not even be believed by outsiders. At times, it seemed like the hand of God would be responsible for hilarious moments. One rainy afternoon, we happened to be dealing with a difficult guest. She was on stage rehearsing, and as everyone was gingerly working through the uncomfortable atmosphere she'd established, water began leaking from the roof, due to the storm outside. Someone called the man in charge of the facilities to report the problem, and he happened to approach me as I stood with the crew. "Hey Ed, someone said there's a drip in the studio?"

I pointed to the difficult guest and said, "Yep. There she is." Everyone laughed, and I thought, wow, only a divine providence would actually set up an exchange like that in real life.

I do recall a few other gifts like that from the universe. I was once dictating some copy to a Writers Assistant as he typed it into his computer. The host of the show happened to be a very vulgar guy, lots of bad language off-air. As the assistant was typing, he had a computer glitch, and said, "I can't find the cursor!" And I said, "Oh, he's probably in his dressing room." Another delicious eephus pitch from the great Comedy Producer in the sky.

As I'm thinking about it, one more: while working on a short-lived series involving a difficult, mean-spirited host, the network was concerned about language on the show, specifically, the F word. Even though we were on cable, they wanted to keep the profanity at a minimum. But the host seemingly didn't care and tended to add expletives for no apparent reason to the material we wrote. During a rehearsal, as the host stood on stage dropping swear words, a network exec sidled up to me and whispered, "How many fucks is that?" And I said, "Counting the one on stage telling the jokes, that's six."

Another phenomenon of Hollywood is how people treat each other at the workplace. Personally, I've always believed in being nice to everyone, regardless of who was above who on the supposed food chain. As a writer, performer, and producer, I was considered "above the line" on shows, which technically meant I was one of the muckety-mucks, but I never cared much about that, other than how it was reflected in my paychecks. One season, Dennis got a new assistant. Let's call her Kristen, since that's her name. She seemed nice, a friendly young woman we'd always chat with. She would field Dennis's phone calls, help with his schedule, run errands for him, and also help the writers out when needed, such as getting us source material for a topic we were working on. She was always pleasant to deal with. Then, Dennis went off to shoot a movie for a few weeks in Vancouver, and he took his assistant Kristen with him. She had never been on a movie set before, and of course being with a celebrity like Dennis, she was treated a bit more specially than other crew members. (Not that it's right, but that's how things go.)

We were all happy to have Dennis back at work after the movie wrapped. But the person who came back with him, we didn't really recognize. Somehow, Kristen had developed an attitude that *she* was a star, and started talking down to everyone around her, even though we technically outranked her. It was so uncomfortable. The only thing more pathetic than a celebrity mistreating people is an *assistant* to a celebrity mistreating people. And it's sadly common in Hollywood. You think stars are insecure and insufferable? Try dealing with their "entourage." And often, the stars don't even know that people that are supposed to be representing them are out there behaving like horses' asses.

Some of these gatekeepers don't even pass things along to their boss. They'll reject copy and make demands and present it as if it's all coming from the talent themselves. It used to be the agents and managers who behaved in

9

this fashion, but these days, many publicists have assumed this role. I can't tell you how many times I've written copy for a star to recite on an awards show, and had the publicist send it back with insulting feedback saying her boss hates it. Then later, I approach the star directly when I see them and offer up the "rejected" idea, and they love it, which clearly indicates they never saw the idea in the first place. (More on that later.)

But now, back to our story. One of Kristen's jobs had always been to keep the conference room table organized, cleared of mail and the many magazines and newspapers we got every day to help with our research. Things would stack up as runners would drop off wire photos and publications. The writers would pick them up and use them as needed, then would drop them back at the table for others to use. At the end of each day, Kristen would put the old items into filing cabinets, and the table would be free for the next day's batch of material, as well as being clear for the next morning's meeting. But after apparently being knighted as royalty during her movie adventure, Kristen deemed the task of keeping the source materials organized as completely beneath her, so she simply didn't do it. We'd politely ask for her help as the table became more unwieldy, but she'd respond that she was "too busy," as she sat at her desk, a few feet away from the growing trash heap, reading a romance novel. Seriously. After a week or so, the entire room had become a fire hazard. Despite our best efforts at doing Kristen's job for her, we also had our own jobs to do, which was to write comedy on a deadline every day, so things continued to pile up.

One morning I came in to the offices before everyone else (which I frequently did, because I loved the peace and quiet so conducive to writing) and I had a "Popeye" attack. No, not the desire for spinach, or fast food chicken, but the attitude of "I can't stands it no more!" and I scooped up everything on the table and stacked it on Kristen's empty desk. Actually, I more "heaved it" rather than stacked it, hurling heavy loads of *The Hollywood Reporter* like the guys who throw huge fish around at that Seattle market. It looked like two newsstands had just been dropped out of the sky by a tornado.

Unfortunately, as I was doing so, one of the producers walked into the room and quite understandably was aghast at what was taking place. As I started to explain, I realized that really, there was no good explanation for any of it. But at least we had a clean table for that morning's meeting.

One of the head studio folks finally had a talk with Kristen, and she reluctantly went back to doing her job (in between chapters of *The Shirtless Hunk and the Princess.*)

*   *   *   *

Among the staff of a typical TV show, there are more than a small amount of shall we say, "eccentric" personalities flitting about. This is especially true in the entry level job of a production, formally known as "Production Assistants," but are colloquially referred to as "PAs," "runners," or "nephews/nieces of executives." They are essentially gophers, and of course there's nothing wrong with that, it's actually a very important part of any production. It's somewhat the equivalent of starting in the mailroom, if it was legal to smoke pot in the mailroom. For people who take the position seriously, it's a great way to learn about the inner workings of a TV show, and to gain valuable experience, as well as foster connections and be mentored. Many folks have used being a PA as a springboard into their own successful careers as writers, producers, actors, editors, etc.

Of course, as I imagine happens in any line of work, there are those who take these positions reluctantly, almost in disgust, certain that they already know far more than any of the people in charge. (Admittedly, they actually sometimes *do* know more than the people in charge. But that's not my point.)

And I'm not sure if I actually do have a point, other than it never ceased to amaze me that people just beginning to work in a business could have such entitled attitudes from the very start. Examples:

- An Executive Producer asked a PA to make a fresh pot of coffee, which is totally in keeping with the job's duties. The PA actually said to him, "The writers can make their own coffee!" and stormed away from his boss. Actually, the EP was *everyone's* boss. The EP looked shocked, and saw that I'd overseen this bit of workplace magic. He chuckled, and said to me "I guess you writers can make your own coffee!" I said, "Of course. You should have told him, "You're right, they can. So, what do we need you for? You're fired!""

- You remember those pictures I mentioned earlier that we had to caption on *Dennis Miller Live*? (Or maybe you only remember the pictures I accidentally left on the fridge. I know I'm still trying to forget about those.) Anyway, there was a PA in charge of photocopying and delivering a batch of the latest wire service pictures to each writer every day. Let me say right here: to me, there's three different kinds of people in the world; 1) Funny people who know they're funny, 2) Funny people who don't know they're funny, and 3) People who think they're funny yet don't have a funny bone in their body. I'm talking so unfunny that the actual humerus bone doesn't even exist in their skeletal structure. Unfortunately, the "picture delivery" PA fell into the third category. He was constantly wandering through the writing offices, and as Kevin Rooney perfectly put it, "Rattling his bad jokes like Jacob Marley's chains." We'd all just smile and nod politely, as one might do if accosted by a screaming indigent in the streets, figuring it was the price we had to pay to have our source material delivered to us.

One afternoon, I noticed we still hadn't received the day's photos, and considering we had to present our jokes in a meeting in a few hours, I became concerned. I went to the production offices to see what the holdup was. I arrived to find "Jacob Marley" calmly captioning photos at his cubicle. "Hey, how's it going?"

"Good. What can I do for you, Ed?"

"Well, I noticed we don't have our photos yet, and we have to pitch our stuff later today."

"Oh yeah, we have the photos. I've just been too busy captioning some of my own to pitch to you guys."

Well. Okay then. I wasn't sure what to say next, but I tried anyway. "Uh, can the writers get our copies, too?" He smiled and shrugged. "Well, yes, hopefully later today when I'm done working on *my* batch." Once I was able to locate a pulley system to pick my jaw up off the floor, I made my way to the Head Writer's office. I hated feeling like I was going to the teacher to tattle, but I honestly didn't know what else to do. I thought, well, maybe the Head Writer actually asked the PA to contribute some of his own material? But when it took me nearly fifteen minutes to convince the Head Writer I wasn't making the whole "I'm captioning my own" story up, it became clear he hadn't asked the PA to submit his own material after all. Following a quick, awkward call that I had to witness, a chastened Jacob Marley appeared, tossing the photos onto everyone's desk with nary a bad joke to be told. He shot me a dirty look, and left, no doubt, to go back to the bad jokes of Christmas past.

- In one of my previous books, *Spilled Gravy*, I told the story of being a Producer and Head Writer on a show and walking into my office one day to discover the guy that was supposed to be fixing my computer was actually sitting at my desk, pen in hand, writing suggestions onto my script!! That's still the most brazen display I've seen (so far.)

- On another sitcom I worked on, one of the production executives asked a PA to deliver lunch to the creative team. The PA replied, "I have better things to do than get the producers lunch." Um actually, you don't. It's your job. To quote the great Foghorn Leghorn, "That boy had more nerve than a bum tooth." I wish I had that kind of audacity. Alas, I can only fantasize about barking "Hey, I've got better things to do than write scripts!" at my boss.

* * * *

With many of the PAs on Dennis's show, there was nothing that irritated them more than being asked to do their jobs. Every day we got copies of *USA Today* delivered to our offices, a great resource for writing jokes. It covers the news at a mostly superficial level, so one can read just far enough into the story to get some jokes, then you can move on. (When I was on Dennis's show, because we did so much topical humor, people assumed I knew all the big news happenings in depth. I always had to explain, my knowledge is more miles wide and inches deep, because I'd read as much as I needed to get some comedy gold, then I was finished with the topic and on to the next story.)

At any rate, something went awry one day with our morning newspaper delivery, and Greg the writer called a PA named Brian to ask if he'd go somewhere nearby and grab some copies of *USA Today* for the writers. We remembered that the studio commissary always received a stack in the morning, perhaps they'd gotten their delivery today? Brian said he had already stopped by the commissary and that they were sold out. (And apparently, leaving the studio lot to buy it nearby was out of the question for him.) After Greg hung up with Brian, I said, "Boy, that seems strange to me. They usually get a ton of copies in the commissary, especially considering how early it is. Maybe we should go down and check."

So Greg and I sauntered across the lot and into the commissary, where we immediately saw about thirty copies of *USA Today* for sale. Obviously, Brian had just been too lazy to take a five-minute walk to check the commissary, but he made up for his sloth by being a bald-faced liar.

Greg and I laughed about it, purchased a bunch of copies, and brought them back to our offices. We didn't even think about calling Brian back, what would be the point? He'd just make up some other crazy story, and unlike Brian, we just wanted to do our jobs.

Later that afternoon, as we all were in our offices writing, Brian showed up to drop off the day's photos for captioning. I sat at my desk chuckling to myself about the newspaper incident from that morning, and thought well, Brian is lucky he works with nice people. Suddenly, Greg's voice rang out from his office, "Well, well!! If it isn't Lyin' Brian!!" The look on Brian's face was priceless. Google the word "busted," and you'll see his expression. Poor Brian tried to feign surprise, as though he didn't know what Greg was talking about. But when Greg emerged from his office smirking, holding a *USA Today*, Brian knew he was toast. I emerged from my office with my *USA Today*, and suddenly so did the next writer, and the next writer. Obviously, we were *all* Spartacus. Brian stammered some kind of lame excuse and hurried out. I'm guessing that while this incident didn't prevent him from lying in the future, I'll bet he at least learned to tell lies that aren't so easily debunked.

Sometimes the PA's attitudes weren't actually pernicious, just clueless. Writer Bill Braudis's mother-in-law passed away during our first season, and everyone on the production was sad to hear this news. Since Bill was a close friend of mine, I told the producers I'd arrange for a sympathy card, and make sure everyone got to sign it before we gave it to Bill. I discreetly phoned a PA named Sebastian and said, "Hi, can you get me a sympathy card for Bill?"

He said, "Sure." About an hour later, I'm sitting in my office with my door open, and Bill happened to be standing in the hallway. Imagine my horror when Sebastian marched up to Bill and said, "Here, I was supposed to get a sympathy card for you?" and handed it to him. I caught Sebastian's eye and furiously gestured for him to bring it to *me*, not Bill. Bill turned and saw me, and realizing what had just happened, he burst out laughing. We continue to laugh about it to this day. The rogue PA still didn't realize what he'd done, and merely shrugged and handed the card to me and left.

Sebastian was also infamous for barging into people's offices unannounced. I would think even a bull might give a light tap with its horns first before storming in. This guy never met a closed door that he didn't burst through without knocking. It was really quite unnerving. Usually, we left our office doors open, mostly because we wanted to hear what kind of funny nonsense might suddenly erupt in the common area, which happened frequently. Some of the funniest conversations I've ever heard and/or been part of happened in that space. Someone would bring up something happening in the news, then someone else would recount some weird personal story from their day, and the next thing you knew there was a bunch of hilarious people swapping stories, making up song parodies, doing physical shtick. Hilarious and entertaining stuff.

Regarding the normal "open door" policy, it was fun if you didn't want to miss what was happening in the rest of the office. But if one was on a deadline, or really needed to concentrate, we'd close our doors. As mentioned, to Sebastian, a closed door meant nothing other than an opportunity to scare the crap out of you. It was hard not to flinch when you'd be buried in thought and suddenly the door would fling wide open as if someone had planted a dynamite charge, and he'd toss some papers on your desk and be gone. Whenever someone would ask him to please knock before entering, he'd get that same confused look that well, to be honest, that he pretty much wore 24/7. So at least he was consistent.

This became a fun game for all of us, because whenever we saw Sebastian arrive, we quickly looked to see who had their door closed, then we'd eagerly gather outside that office to watch the PA scare the hell out of his latest victim. It was like hanging out at a Halloween haunted house just to watch people be startled near to death. As he'd enter someone's office, I'd loudly yell "Barge!!!" and we'd all laugh. I know, a sad excuse for entertainment. But please don't begrudge us our little joys in life. We had all kinds of fun with it. *"Knock Knock. Who's there? Well, it can't be Sebastian."*

Alas, the "barge" era eventually came to an end, but it went out in fine fashion. One day, Dennis was meeting with all the very top executives of HBO, to discuss the future of the show. It was quite the gathering of power elites, and as they filed into Dennis's office and closed the door, we all sat in the conference area, nervously speculating. Were we going to be cancelled? Picked up? Picked up, then cancelled? We were a critical and popular hit by that point, but that often means nothing with the capricious whims of the entertainment industry.

As we fidgeted and swapped stories, in swept Hurricane Sebastian, carrying a bag of food, evidently Dennis's lunch. "Dennis in here?" he asked, and before we could finish saying, "Yeah, but he's meeting with—" he flung open the door to Dennis's office and charged in as unobtrusively as a sumo wrestler playing the bagpipes. All we heard was the familiar tones of Dennis shouting, "What the fuck?!" and seconds later, Sebastian came back out, for the first time in his life looking a bit sheepish. We felt very privileged to be witnesses to what was apparently the first instance of self-awareness he'd experienced in his twenty-one years on the planet, and when he looked at us, we stood and applauded. He smiled, muttered, "Guess I should have knocked, maybe," and disappeared down the hall, taking the legend of "Large Barge" off into the sunset with him.

*　　*　　*　　*

I'll be the first to say I detest the abusive, egomaniacal blowhards too often found in Hollywood. However, I'm also the first to say, nothing is funnier to me than *pretending* to be an abusive, egomaniacal blowhard in Hollywood. Let me explain. Once people get to know me, I always like to put on the character of the demanding jerk, dismissing everyone around me as lowly servants. It's just a character I break into occasionally to entertain my coworkers. A favorite affectation is to dismiss anyone "underneath" me as a "shithead." I'll bark, "I need my lunch, send a shithead over to take my order!" or "Have my shithead call your shithead to set up a meeting!" and so forth. I'll admit,

17

I especially like to refer to the PAs as shitheads, only because it seems particularly condescending (again, in character.) Of course, doing something like this seems almost certain to come back to bite you, and it's happened more than once.

One of my favorites was when a terrific, sweet-natured woman named Colleen, who worked on *DML*, approached me quietly and said, "Ed, I know you're just joking, but it's really not nice referring to people as 'shitheads' behind their backs." I felt chastened, and I told her she was right, and I'd stop doing it.

About a week later, I was in the hallway at the studios and I overheard Colleen having an increasingly aggravated phone conversation, her voice slowly rising as the call went on. Suddenly she shouted, "Just do it, you shithead!!" and slammed the phone down. I walked over and stuck my head into her office, and the second she saw me she burst into laughter. I said, "Oh, now I understand, you were saying don't call people shitheads to their backs, do it to their *faces!*" She laughed, and explained that she was merely asking a PA to do his job, and he called her a bitch. Seriously. I figured something big must have happened for her to lose it like that, but it's still one of our favorite moments to reminisce about. Unsurprisingly, I went back to routinely referring to several of the PAs as shitheads, and Colleen did not object, regardless of whether I was doing so in "character" or not!

My other favorite "shithead" story occurred when I was writing on a sitcom with my dear friend Brian Scully (*The Simpsons*, *Family Guy*, et al.) Besides being incredibly talented, Brian is one of the nicest people you will ever meet.

We used to have group meetings in the writers room when we were breaking stories for episodes. We'd usually kick ideas around, then when we felt we were onto something solid, we'd call in a Writers Assistant to have them write it up in a new document. Of course, I had brought my whole "shitheads" thing with me from *DML*, and I'd always ask the EP, "Should I call a shithead in now?" He'd laugh and if he said "Yes", I'd pick up the room phone and call the production office. Often as I was waiting for a Writers Assistant to answer, I'd pretend as though they'd already picked up, and I'd say, "Yeah, send a shithead over." People would laugh then realize nobody had answered yet. At least, *most* everyone realized nobody had answered, and I was just goofing around.

One day, the phone had been moved to another part of the conference table, and when we were ready to have a Writers Assistant join us, I said to Brian, "Okay, call in a shithead." So the affable Brian picked up the phone, and after a moment, said "Hi, can one of you shitheads come over now?" There was a pause, then Brian looked surprised, and said, "Um, it's Brian.... yes, we need a Writers Assistant in the room now." There was another pause, then Brian hung up, looking a bit confused. I said, "Did you actually say that to them?" He said, "Yeah! I thought you always called them that." I hung my head. "No! I was always saying that before they answered, I never called them that!" Brian and I both looked embarrassed, and of course the rest of the room was roaring with laughter. Then, in came one of the Writers Assistants. He was laughing and shaking his head, saying, "Wow, that's not right!" So I was put in the delicate situation of explaining to all the Writers Assistants that I would never call them shitheads to their face, only behind their backs!! Which of course, only sounds worse!! Once I explained it to them, it became the running gag of the show. I'd see a Writers Assistant in the hallway, and he/she would say, "So, do you assholes need one of us shitheads in the room yet?" And mind you, this was all on a kid's show! To this day, my good friend David Vallierre, who I met on that show when he was a Writers' Assistant, leaves me messages saying "Hey, it's the number one shithead. Give me a call."

Another favorite "angry celebrity' character to quote is that of the famous drummer Buddy Rich. There is a legendary recording of him berating his bandmembers in the most profane, belittling, yet irresistibly hilarious manner one could imagine. And you didn't have to imagine, because obviously these rants were so common that his band began surreptitiously recording his outbursts, and these made their way around the subculture of show biz via cassettes starting in the late 1980s. It was quite the underground hit, though now it's easily findable on the internet, and thus kinda feels like it's lost its "insider" luster. Interestingly, Damien Chazelle, who wrote the movie *Whiplash*, admitted that the main protagonist — played so brilliantly by J.K. Simmons that he won an Oscar for it — was based on his own abusive music teacher, as well as the rants of Buddy Rich from the legendary tapes.

There are so many great lines from Mr. Rich's rants, and I love to quote them constantly, especially around other comics and writers. Once while writing on the ESPN *Espys* sports awards show, I was backstage entertaining my fellow scribes by going full-on Buddy on them. Unbeknownst to me, several ESPN executives were walking down the hall, and heard my cries of "I'm working my fucking balls off to do somebody a favor, and you mother-fuckers are sucking all over this joint! Assholes! You're all a bunch of fucking children!" wafting out of the writers room. Understandably horrified, they went to the Producer of the show and said, "Somebody in there is cursing out everybody on the staff in a very inappropriate manner." And the Producer simply said, "What? Oh, that's Ed" and offered no further explanation. I didn't find out about this conversation until days after it occurred, and only then did I understand why the executives always gave me a nervous look whenever they saw me.

On another occasion, I was working with the talented Jay Mohr. He was hosting the 2011 NHL Awards, and I was helping him write his open-ing monologue. Jay is a large personality for sure, and a very funny guy. He was a fan of the Buddy Rich tirades just like me, and we'd often break into the various rants to amuse ourselves. Generally, we did this backstage, but during the biggest rehearsal on the day before the show, we started "argu-ing," using various Buddy lines, right onstage in front of everyone. Most of the crew knew we were kidding, but some folks, particularly the executives from the network, as well as the NHL suits, had no frame of reference as to what was happening. So I'm shouting at Jay, "What the hell is wrong with you? Miscue after miscue!" and he's shouting back "I've got a right hand for your fucking brain, if you want it!" Unbeknownst to us, a few folks from the NHL approached the producer to tell him that there was a horrible argument breaking out on the set. (You know you've stepped overboard when people from the world of professional hockey find your behavior too abusive and threatening.)

Another little story from that show: as Jay and I crafted the monologue, we included a joke making fun of one of the hockey franchises that was really struggling financially at the time. While the NHL executives had given us a lot of leeway, they were very sensitive about this particular topic, and one of them, John Collins, came into my office one day for a chat. I like John, a sharp, affable guy. He used to work for the NFL, and I knew him from some shows I'd done for the football folks as well. John expressed his concern about the financial hardship joke, and I understood his point. And more importantly, I understood that he signed our paychecks for this show, and I told him I'd speak to Jay about it.

Just before rehearsal, I stopped by Jay's dressing room and told him about my talk with John. Jay shrugged and said "Yeah, it's a really funny joke, but I understand. We're long anyway, so let's just cut the joke." I agreed, and went to the teleprompter and removed the joke from the script.

I took my seat in the theater to watch rehearsal of the opening monologue, and John took a seat next to me. I assured him I'd talked to Jay and that we were totally cool, the joke is out of the show. John expressed his appreciation, and the Director began rehearsal and Jay walked out on stage. He ran through the jokes flawlessly, all the execs laughing, a good sign. Then suddenly, Mohr did "the" joke that we had supposedly cut. The execs immediately turned and looked at me, and I looked back at them, just as stunned as they were, and threw up my hands. I looked back at the teleprompter to see if the joke was still in there, and it was not. Jay had merely decided to ad-lib it, (maybe just to fuck with me?) He shot me a smirk from onstage as he saw the execs huddling with me, then continued his rehearsal. I explained to everyone that we had cut it, it was out of the prompter, and that I'd get to the bottom of it.

Of course, when I walked into Jay's dressing room he immediately burst out laughing. He had indeed done the joke just to screw with me, and it was hilarious, I had to admit. He assured me he wouldn't do it during the actual live broadcast, and I told the executives this, but in my mind I really wasn't sure if he'd do it or not, and I gently told them as much. Fortunately for all of us, Jay stuck with the script for the actual show —no forbidden jokes — got big laughs, and we all got our paychecks signed.

*　*　*　*

Honestly, I don't blame executives for being frightened or put off by comics and comedy writers. We do, and say, some weird stuff. And I don't mean like Louie CK weird. Just weird like the Buddy Rich quoting. Or just the bizarre things that we find funny.

There is a legendary video of a comedian named Kenny Moore clobbering a heckler with his guitar, an incident that took place in some club in Oklahoma in the 1980s. It was yet another "underground" hit, literally, and of course is readily viewable on YouTube now. But back in the early 90s, you could only get it from some other comic who dubbed you a copy on VHS. That incident is one of the very best litmus tests to demonstrate the difference between comedians' sense of humor, and that of normal, or "civilian" people, as we often call non-comedians. The first time I saw the tape, with Kenny snapping on a heckler, then leaning into the crowd to blast the poor dude across his skull, then returning to the stage with the back of his guitar busted up, ready to continue the show, I laughed so hard I literally fell out of my chair. I think any performer who has ever had their show interrupted by some stupid drunk finds the tape incredibly cathartic. But any civilian I've ever shown it to was completely horrified, probably understandably. I remember eagerly loading it into the VCR to show my new girlfriend one night, guaranteeing her she'd laugh like crazy, and when she saw it, she burst into tears, calling it the worst thing she's ever seen. I'm guessing the "proper" reaction is something in between that of hers and mine.

At any rate, when *Dennis Miller Live* was just starting production for its first episode, I showed Dennis the Kenny Moore tape, and he of course found it hysterical. In the tape, after Kenny tries to get the crowd back on his side after opening someone's pate like an over-ripe melon, they are, unsurprisingly, not on his side. So he simply says, "Okay, show's over!" and walks offstage. Dennis found the clip so funny, he wanted to use it as the closing credits for our show. Meaning our names would be scrolling down the screen as Kenny hit the heckler, and would end with Kenny saying "Okay, show's over!" So the first thing we had to do was hunt down Kenny, see if he had the original tape, and if so, would he be willing to sell us the legal rights to run the footage each week?

We were able to reach Kenny, and he had quite the story to tell. He was a very nice guy, and he said he'd be happy to let us use it, and didn't even want to be paid. In fact, he offered to send us the actual splintered guitar, the "evil talisman" as he called it. He did so, also enclosing a very funny handwritten note telling the entire story, how he thought he was about to be assaulted, and the heckler ended up not being seriously injured but required stitches — yep, literally had the guy in stitches — and it landed him in jail in Oklahoma for three days. Kenny was ordered to pay for the heckler's medical expenses and court costs. He also was told he couldn't perform in Oklahoma ever again, though I doubt he was very dismayed with that part of the sentencing.

When the package arrived, Dennis gleefully had the main body of the guitar mounted on a plaque and hung on his office wall. I asked for the remaining shards from the back of the guitar, and still have them today. We laid out a track of our proposed ending credits, and excitedly screened them for the HBO executives. As had happened with my girlfriend, they did not quite see the humor, appropriateness, or connection whatsoever of putting this particular piece of mayhem at the end of their brand new show, and politely put the whole notion to rest.

I have to admit, the executives were absolutely right. The clip really had no context other than "show's over!" and would've been a terrible ending for every viewer in the country who wasn't a twisted comedian. And as we sputtered our reasons for why this would be a great show ending to the pantheon of confused and somewhat distressed bosses, we started to realize we had made an embarrassing misjudgment. And after the execs left, we had quite a laugh at our own expense, shaking our heads at what the hell we could have been thinking.

However, there was one weird, out of context reference to another underground video clip that we did manage to get on the show, on every episode in fact. In the early 90s, there was a tape of some obscure, bad comedian doing horrible material at some dingy little club. The tape was popular because it was so bad on so many levels, and thus had become a cult classic amongst comedians and other folks of our ilk. At the very beginning of the tape, as he walked on stage, the comic shouted out, "What's happening, Cleveland!" I had showed the tape to Dennis, which of course he enjoyed, and we started greeting each other every day with "What's happening, Cleveland!" Then on the night of the first show, broadcast live across the country, Dennis walked out to the applause and suddenly said, "What's happening, Cleveland!" The entire staff was surprised and delighted by this obscure homage. The audience just laughed because well, they figured he was saying something funny. Which he was, but not for any reasons they would know. And thus began the tradition of opening every show with the immortal words, "What's happening, Cleveland!" It was even loaded into the teleprompter each week, just to make sure Dennis didn't forget to say it. (Since Dennis is from Pittsburgh, as am I, people back there were constantly asking us why he didn't greet his old hometown instead of the "rival" town, but we simply explained, "inside joke.")

* * * *

There was always something interesting happening at historic CBS Television City. We were surrounded by shows more famous than ours, most notably, *The Price Is Right*. As you may know, *The Price Is Right* really relies on the folks who sit in the audience to generate the excitement, because they are the ones who are randomly called to "Come on down!" and be contestants on the show. People would start lining up in the street and in the CBS parking lot in the early morning hours just for a chance to attend the taping and perhaps even win some prizes. It was quite a spectacle of humanity, which was somewhat entertaining, but the annoying part was, people seemed to have no qualms about parking in spots that were clearly marked "Dennis Miller Live Staff Only," and we'd often be stuck driving around looking for another place to park on the lot. We asked the security guards to be more vigilant about this, but for whatever reason they seemed more concerned about the *Price Is Right* folks than us folks that actually worked on the lot. It was amazing how often I'd arrive at my parking spot only to find a giant wood-paneled station wagon with Colorado plates and Cracker Barrel decals already parked there. I always had the initial fear that it was the car of someone hired to replace me.

Often during coffee breaks, we'd wander around the studio lot, dodging various forklifts and golf carts whizzing around the cavernous backstage halls, and gawk at the flashy sets of other shows such as *Wheel of Fortune*. We'd fantasize about sneaking in and putting obscene words into the puzzles, just to surprise the viewers. Though most of us were in our late 20s/early 30s, we did tend to behave like sixth-graders when we were in any group of two or more. (Incidentally, it wasn't just the guys, the female writers were equally invested in juvenile behavior.) I suppose I could try to excuse some of the behavior by saying it was really all a way to blow off steam. Which is true, but it's also true that being goofy was simply very, very fun.

On one show I worked on, the host was mean to everyone, and was driving everybody crazy. But the show was just a one-time deal, not a series,

25

so knowing that it was coming to an end shortly made things a bit more palatable. (In that same vein, there's a famous story in Hollywood about Martin Lawrence basically torturing everyone involved during the shooting of his movie, *What's The Worst That Could Happen?* When the crew received t-shirts with the movie title on the front, they added the words "A Sequel!" to the back.)

Anyhow, as a way of coping with the ridiculous demands of the host, it became a popular game amongst the staff to joke about murdering said host, then desecrating the corpse. It was only in jest...mostly. (I know, right now I'm betting you have that same expression "civilians" have when I show them the Kenny Moore video. Or, maybe you're laughing, to which I say, you must be a comedian friend of mine, and thanks for reading my book, though you're probably just reading it to see if I mention you by name.) Another writer and I invented a little "Improv" type of troupe (though it was just he and I) which we called "The Desecration Players." We would stroll unannounced into someone's office, then using no words, we'd pantomime various homicide/corpse abuse scenarios, then join hands, bow deeply as if acknowledging a cheering crowd, and exit without a word. People started leaving their office doors open all the time, hoping we'd drop by and give a little performance. At one point, we started feeling more pressure to make these little skits funny than we did to make the host's show material funny.

Another fun thing I did on that particular show: I had a "crowd cheer" audio clip on my computer, and whenever that particular host would leave the offices, I'd play it loudly so that everyone could hear a crowd cheering the exit of this pain in the ass. Of course, once again I was playing with fire, and one time as I had cranked up the cheers, the host suddenly came back into the offices to retrieve something they'd forgotten. They heard this loud roar of approval coming from my computer, and asked me "What's that?" "Um, I'm just checking some clips of your past performances!" I lied. This seemed to appease them, and they left. Whew, that was close. I'd learned my lesson. Which meant next time, I waited a solid 30 seconds after the host had left before launching the robust computer-generated ovation.

Working for truly abusive and/or difficult hosts is never fun, and most sane people would rather work with nice folks. The only bright spot in working with jerks was that it tended to bring the crew closer together, in an "us versus him/her" kind of way. Writers that maybe wouldn't get along so well in normal working circumstances tend to bond in the bunker mentality that forms at a show involving difficult talent. A couple quick examples:

I was writing/consulting on a one-off, live variety special, and the host was — stop me if you've heard this before — difficult. As the writers would discuss the jokes they'd written for him, he would often talk over them and add his own rewrite of the joke, which was inevitably way worse than the version that had been pitched to him. Everyone realized there was no use in arguing with this person, he wasn't really interested in feedback, he just wanted to do everything his own way, and we were resigned to it. It's a frustrating position to be in when you're a professional, because you want the show to be as good as it can be, and it's weird when you feel like you care more about the show than the person whose name is on it does. I'm sure I'm not shocking you when I say that lots of people in Hollywood only want ass-kissers on their staff, and don't want to hear anything except confirmation of their own genius. On the other hand, I've been lucky to work with people like Dennis Miller, Billy Crystal, and others who are secure enough in their own talent that they want to hear honest feedback about their material, because they want the finished product to be as good as it can be. They realize that someone like me isn't pushing back on a joke or idea because I want to be difficult, but because I, too, care about the show, and want to offer my best, honest opinions about what we need to get us to the best place we can be. At any rate, this particular show was the polar opposite of all that, and at one point, one of the writers, let's call him Ernie, had written a really brilliant joke that everyone loved. Everyone except the host, that is, either because he wasn't smart enough to understand the line, or just always figured all his

27

lines are better than anyone else's (probably both.) So he changed the line to something really unfunny and juvenile, and that's how it went into the script.

After the writing session broke up, several of us approached Ernie to offer our condolences for his great writing being ruined, and he shrugged it off. He said, "Well, I'm hoping he'll re-think it, and put it back into the script in its original form. He has to realize the version he came up with is embarrassing." I wasn't as optimistic about this, but wasn't about to convey it at that moment.

A few days later, the show was set to air, live across the country. As it turned out, poor Ernie had had to have emergency dental surgery that morning, and understandably he missed the rehearsals. In fact, nobody expected to see him at the show that evening considering what he'd gone through. He'd already earned his pay, and pretty much all the real behind-the-scenes work was finished.

That night, about five minutes before the show was to go live, me and another writer named David were sitting backstage, ready to watch the show unfold on the monitors. Right as it began, we were quite surprised when Ernie showed up, face swollen to pumpkin dimensions, obviously in pain and just as obviously still a bit doped up from the anesthesia. "Hey, what are you doing here? You must feel terrible!" I said, but he dismissed my concerns, and said he just wanted to see how the show went tonight. I told him he could have watched at home, but he dismissed that idea as well. He asked, "Did he change that joke back to the good version?" "Unfortunately," I answered, "he's going with the stupid one. What can you do?" Ernie stood silently for a moment, then announced, "Well, I'm going into the audience area. And if he does that joke, I'm going to boo." And with that he left the backstage area. David and I looked at each other and cracked up. We figured, no way he'd really do that, right? Nah. No way. He was just being funny.

We sort of forgot about the whole exchange while we were watching the show. Everything was going smoothly, the audience was responsive to the jokes, which made us look good. Then, the host did "the joke," the bad version of Ernie's joke. It got a small laugh, but not nearly as big of a response as the other jokes had been getting. This didn't surprise us because we knew it was weak. What *did* surprise us however, was that right after the host finished the punchline, we heard a loud "booo!" ring through the audience. We realized immediately Ernie had gone through with his promise. The host stopped for just a second, looking a little surprised, then merely went on with the next joke. It was one of the most incredible things I've witnessed in my career. David and I were laughing so hard, I thought I was going to wet my pants. Hell, I thought I was going to wet David's pants. As we found out later, Ernie had indeed wandered into the studio as the show was broadcasting live, then hid under the audience bleachers, waiting for his moment. He launched his scornful salvo, then strolled out of the studio and went home, to sleep off the rest of the anesthesia.

The next day, I got a call from one of the Producers, who asked me if I knew anything about Ernie's antics. Even though I consider myself to be a very honest person, there was no way I was going to sell Ernie out, so I feigned total ignorance about the whole thing. The Producer then said to me, "Well, if we do another one of these shows, I'm going to have to ask the writers not to boo during the telecast." Awesome. Now there's the sign of a well-run show, when the person in charge feels obligated to tell the writing staff to please not boo the host on live television.

In a semi-related note, on one other show I worked on, with, yet again, a difficult host, me and one of the writers made a game of standing in the audience as the show was taping, appearing to be smiling and applauding. But we'd actually groan and hiss occasionally through our supposedly smiling teeth. We'd see the host glance around to see where it was coming from, but all he saw when he looked at us was a couple supportive, applauding, smiling writers. I know, what can I say? Shameful and unprofessional, but hilarious. I defy anyone to tell me otherwise.

Please don't get the wrong idea, that I'm some insane, rebellious guy whenever I work on shows. These stories I'm telling you are certainly outliers. A large percentage of hosts and actors I've worked with have been terrific. And while I am never shy about offering my opinion on something to people above me, I also never hesitate to do my very best to execute their wishes, whether they take my advice on something or not. I have my honest say, and again, I only speak up because I believe I'd be doing people that hire me a disservice to not give my honest opinion. But once I've given that opinion, and if they don't agree, I salute and fall in line, and work hard to make their choice work. I've seen writers who, after offering their two cents, continue to argue their point, then sometimes sulk about it. Not helpful, not a good look, and not a good hire. Those people generally stop getting work due to an intransigent reputation.

Okay, back to CBS Television City and Dennis's show. Our *DML* offices were right next to the studio and offices for legendary talk show host Tom Snyder. We'd see him often, and he always gave a friendly greeting, but all I could ever think of was Dan Akroyd's hilarious impression of him on *Saturday Night Live*. Akroyd had him down perfectly; the staccato laugh, the head movements, the ever-present blazing cigarette. Speaking of which, in 1995 California was really cutting down on smoking indoors, especially office buildings. So technically, Snyder was not allowed to smoke inside the studio offices anymore. But he got around this decree by leaning out his office window and lighting up, like a teenager trying to smoke pot without his parents knowing. The windows didn't open fully, so he'd have to twist his lower torso and be basically hanging the upper half of his body upside down out the window to enjoy his cigarette. It was always a funny and surreal scene to walk through the courtyard outside and see him hanging out the window, enveloped in white smoke, as if he was announcing the selection of a new

Pope. Why he didn't merely step outside into the courtyard itself to abide his habit, only he knows.

Speaking of smoking, I was still smoking at the time (thankfully I quit in 1995) and since I didn't have the Cirque du Soleil-like flexibility that Mr. Snyder possessed, I'd simply sit outside the building to light up. Weird, I know. Anyway, my smoke breaks often coincided with those of Penn Gillette, the "talking" half of the wonderful magician duo of Penn & Teller. No great story here, other than it was always really nice to chat with him. And as so often happens amongst artists, we never discussed show business stuff, we always just chatted about life. Most of us in the entertainment industry feel smothered by "the biz" a good deal of the time, and are usually grateful for the chance to talk about *anything* else.

There's no doubt that we had our share of interesting people as guests on Dennis's show. It's where I first met Robin Williams. As years went by, I got to know Robin better as I did a lot of work for his buddy Billy Crystal, and his manager David Steinberg (much more on them later!) and eventually did some writing for Robin as well. Robin once sent me a bottle of champagne as a "thank you" after a project we'd done together, and while I didn't drink the champagne (being sober for a long time), I did keep the note that came with it. Whenever I come across the note now stored in a desk drawer, it's quite bittersweet.

On *DML*, we booked all kinds of great and not so great guests, a whirl-wind of celebrities and pundits. I have lots of fleeting memories of many of them. Charlie Sheen, who seemed incredibly fragile and nervous before his appearance (after all, it was live), nervously puffing a cigarette in the hallway before being introduced. Norm MacDonald reducing everyone, including Dennis, to hysterics with his incredibly irreverent diatribes, both on-stage and off. Me freaking out about some change we had to make at the last minute on the "Rant" portion of the show, and dashing into an elevator with another writer, not paying attention to anyone that was already in there, and fretting aloud about the Rant until I looked up and saw Jerry Seinfeld with a big grin on his face. I was embarrassed by how I'd been carrying on and hadn't even noticed him, and I knew him a bit from haunting the same standup clubs. I sheepishly said, "Oh, hi Jerry." And he laughed and asked with mock seriousness, "Hey, how's "The Rant," Ed? Is everything okay? Should I call a doctor?!'"

A couple fun Jerry Seinfeld asides: The very first time I met him was at the LA Improv in the early '90s. I was still anchored in Boston and was just visiting Los Angeles at the time, and was staying with a friend. I was excited to meet Jerry of course, one of the greatest comics of our generation. I nervously did my set that night, then after the show I began walking the 15 blocks or so to my friend's apartment. Suddenly a car passing by honked, and I looked over to see it was Jerry waving at me. He pulled over and offered me a ride, which I gladly accepted. Pretty cool of him.

A few years later, after I'd first moved to LA, I was at the Improv again, looking at notes before my set. The great thing about doing standup in LA is that you never know who's going to drop by to do a quick guest performance. Lots of big stars are constantly working on material, and will come by unannounced to try stuff out, to the surprise and delight of the customers. But it's a double-edged sword if you're also on the bill, and you suddenly find yourself following some incredibly famous act. It happens, and while it can be nerve-wracking, it's a neat experience overall. Anyway, that night as I was sitting in the dressing room, the emcee approached and said, "Hey, there's a quick guest set right before you go on, so hang tight." "Okay," I said nonchalantly. "Anyone I know?" "Seinfeld." Oh boy.

I walked out into the bar area, just outside the showroom, and I saw Jerry hanging out. Since I had met him a few times by that point, I'd figured I'd go tease him. I approached and said, "Seriously, Jerry. You're not successful enough as it is, you need to come down and step on us little guys?" Without missing a beat, he said, "Hey, what do you think the most fun part of being successful is? It's stepping on guys like you!" Hilarious. Anyway, back to adventures at Dennis's show.

When *Dennis Miller Live* was first greenlighted, we were only guaranteed six episodes, and we knew we had to garner favorable publicity quickly in order to convince the network to order more episodes. So naturally, we hired a publicist. Remember, this is before social media, and the job was to get word about our program to as many folks as possible via newspapers, magazines, local and national television, radio, etc. At least, you'd think that was the job, right? None of us were ever quite sure about the publicist we had. He'd show up every few days, ask everyone how it was going, read our copies of the trade papers, then head out. We were bemused by him, and sometimes asked ourselves, "Does he know we have a show on the air?"

Anyway, after our very first show aired, an extremely favorable review appeared in the *New York Times*. The office was abuzz that morning, as copies of the *Times* made their way around, and we were grateful for the positive publicity coup we'd just been handed. Hey, we might not lose our jobs after six shows after all!

As we sat around the conference room chatting excitedly, in strolled our publicist. Figuring he'd been at least partially responsible for getting the review published, we said, "Hey, nice work, great write-up in the *Times*!" He looked puzzled, and said, "What?" We all laughed at his deadpan joke. That is, we laughed until he continued, "What are you guys talking about?" The room got completely silent. Finally, I said, "The great review in today's *New York Times*!" His reply? "I didn't hear about that. Wow, cool. Does anyone have a copy?"

A moment worthy of a *Larry Sanders* episode, except, this was *real*. Goodness. Shockingly, he was fired by the network not long after this. I told Dennis, "Hey, he'll be the last person to read about his firing, maybe we'd better send him a copy of the announcement?"

Publicists are an interesting breed, based on my experience, anyway. Some are terrific at their jobs, and can really help a show or individual artist gain opportunities to introduce themselves to a wider audience. But at some point, many of them tried to usurp agents and managers as the "middlemen" between their clients, and writer-producers.

Usually, if I'm writing a sketch, or presenter patter, or whatever for an actor's appearance on a variety or awards show, I'll speak with the artist directly about what tone they might like to have for their appearance, and work with them to craft something they feel good about performing. Makes sense, right? Well, beginning sometime in the late 1990s, I suddenly found myself grappling with publicists who were running interference for their clients. At first I assumed they were speaking on behalf of the people they represented, because certainly they'd at least show the material to their clients before turning it down, right?

One day while writing for an awards show, after sending several what I considered to be good drafts to an actor, and having them all rejected (at least, according to their publicist), I wondered how this person, who has a reputation as being a really "normal" guy, would suddenly be so picky about all this. I told the publicist over the phone, "Okay, well, I will talk to him tomorrow at rehearsal and find out more of what he's looking for and rewrite it then."

Cut to: the next day, at rehearsal. I approached the actor, and he was as friendly as his reputation suggested he'd be. He politely asked, "Do you have a copy of what I'm supposed to say?" I told him that I was sorry he didn't seem to like what I'd sent him thus far, and that I was eager to craft something he'd be happy with. He gave me a puzzled look.

"You sent me copy already?"

"Um, yeah, several different versions in fact."

"Sorry, I never saw those."

Well, hang on, I told him, and I leafed through my notebook and just happened to have printed copies of the material he'd supposedly rejected. He started reading them, and laughed, then said, "I like them all! Which one do you think I should do?" "Hmm, maybe run them by someone you trust, like maybe, your publicist, and see which one they think you should do," I offered mischievously. Of course, when he did so, the publicist pretended that she'd never seen any of them before, and he ended up doing the version I'd sent on the first try.

Hey, getting feedback from a publicist who apparently wants to be a manager or agent is at least feedback. Nothing's more frustrating than when you send someone's script to them weeks in advance for approval, and while they actually do receive it, they just don't bother to look at it.

The production staff typically makes follow-up calls and sends emails to the artist, to let them know we're close to production time, and if they'd like to add or subtract or completely redo something, now's the time to let us know. But some artists are in such a bubble they don't even know they've received a script, or simply don't care, and show up on set minutes before their appearance and want things completely rewritten immediately.

I've done more last-minute rewrites than I can begin to count, sometimes to the point where the text is still being loaded into the prompter while the talent is actually delivering it to a live audience. Ultimately I don't mind, I'm not the one up there in front of the audience on those occasions, and I get paid the same. But don't get pissy with me if you ignored all our attempts to have you sign off on the copy in advance.

A classic example was a very well-known character actor, who turned out to be quite the "character" indeed. I don't want to say his name, so I'll just call him Dick. He was a presenter at an awards show, alongside an actress he'd never met, which is the sort of thing that happens somewhat frequently at awards shows. Generally, producers like to pair up guests to present different categories, to keep the show moving along. Folks that work on the same show, or even the same network, are easy to place together. They have some familiarity with each other, and often have a nice, natural rhythm they bring from working together previously. But once an awards show is booked, there's always some left over presenters that don't really have a connection, but need to be paired up anyway. It's like a bad dating service. And this can be extremely challenging for everyone involved.

Anyway, Dick hadn't bothered to look at the banter written for him and a young, up and coming actress until about 20 minutes before they were supposed to present it on live television. Dick was obviously smitten by this young actress, and immediately put on airs as if he was Brando, Pacino and DeNiro all rolled into one. Desperately trying not to roll my eyes, I handed them both their pages and asked them if they were satisfied with it. The actress had already read it and was fine with it. But Dick looked at it and literally turned his nose up, and said to me, "This is funny as a root canal!" Before I could stop myself, I said, "Well, saying something is as 'funny as a root canal' is also as funny as said root canal, so let's see what we can do here." He glared at me, and the actress gave me a delighted smirk. Dick's attempt to look like a bigshot in front of the actress hadn't gone quite how he'd expected.

I ended up writing something very straightforward, not really fun at all, but then, that seemed in keeping with his demeanor. I'm happy to note that his behavior is definitely the exception in my experience.

I don't even remember what the copy was, and I'm sure it wasn't anything great, but again, it's why I like the person who will actually be saying it on television to at least look at the script once before coming in to shoot it, or present it live. I'm always happy to make tweaks and rewrites at their direction. After all, they're the ones up there saying it in front of millions of people, so they have a right to be comfortable with it.

When you see some of the lame banter on awards shows, realize that sometimes it's the writers' fault, sometimes it's the presenters' fault, and sometimes, the lack of chemistry is simply too much to overcome. But I say a very sincere *thank you* to actors who are such pros that they get the very most out of a script you've given them.

On one awards show, producers had ended up pairing Noah Wyle and Jeffrey Tambor. As I spoke to each of them, I found out they didn't know each other at all, and in fact, had never met. But they're both true pros, and I tried to think of a fun way for them to introduce their category. On lots of awards shows, you'll see two people who clearly don't know each other, and they usually offer what comes across as insincere, perfunctory praise for each other during their appearance. Knowing the ability of both Wyle and Tambor, I thought it might be fun to put that whole notion on its ear, and wrote them the following:

NOAH WYLE

Thank you, ladies and gentlemen. It's great to be here tonight, and especially exciting to present this award with one of my favorite actors of all time, Jeffrey Tambor.

JEFFREY TAMBOR

Well, thanks! I'm a huge fan of yours, too!

NOAH WYLE

I gotta tell you, I never miss an episode of *Larry Sanders*.

JEFFREY TAMBOR

I appreciate that! And I absolutely love your amazing show, *ER*.

They smile and nod at each other. An awkward pause ensues, then:

NOAH WYLE

You've never seen *ER*, have you?

JEFFREY TAMBOR

Nope. And I'm guessing you've never seen *Larry Sanders*.

NOAH WYLE

No, I don't even know who that is. I don't really know who *you* are.

JEFFREY TAMBOR

Same back at ya. Let's just deliver our lines, collect our checks, and get the hell out of here.

NOAH WYLE

Agreed. Here's the nominees for best dramatic writing…

I was happy that they seemed to "get it," and were willing to give it a try. But I was positively ecstatic when they went out there and just killed it, taking the perfect pause before stating they didn't really know each other, had never seen either person's show, and really just wanted to get through it quickly so they could leave. Writing a fun script, then seeing talented people get the very most out of it, is incredibly satisfying. Score a win for the good guys!

Okay, much more about my adventures writing for awards shows to come, later in the book. Let's "circle back" (as studio execs say to you when they want to blow you off, but I promise, I'm not blowing you, the reader, off. We will actually "circle back.") But first, a few quick mentions of more memorable moments in and around the *Dennis Miller Live* set:

- Much like the previously mentioned incident with the security guard who told me she "liked our pictures," I still cringe from the embarrassment I felt when, one afternoon in the *DML* offices, I was being silly (hard to imagine, I know) and was actually standing on a conference table in the reception area, dancing some crazed version of "the cabbage patch" for the amusement of my co-workers. As everyone laughed, there suddenly was a second wave of huge laughter, and I thought, boy, I'm killing it. And I turned around to see a bemused FedEx delivery guy standing there watching me. I was startled and stopped immediately, whereupon he laughed and said, "Oh, don't stop on my account."

- One day, the lovely and talented actress Sharon Lawrence came by our studio. I always had a crush on her, and when she struck up a conversation with me I couldn't believe my good fortune. The problem was, everybody else in the office knew my feelings as well, and when my phone went off several times as I was talking to her, they enjoyed my fumbling with it and clumsy attempt to silence the ringer. Naturally I found out later that my co-workers were the ones calling me at this inopportune time. Honestly, it was reminiscent of being back in high school, trying to talk to a girl you were interested in in the cafeteria while your friends stood behind her, making faces at you. I guess the classics never age.

*   *   *   *

Around the time I was working on Dennis's show was when I was first introduced to David Steinberg. Not the comedian, the manager. (They even make reference to this on an episode of *Curb Your Enthusiasm*, where every time someone mentions the name "David Steinberg," the other person asks, "The comedian or the manager?") Actually, David is essentially both. He's had a fascinating career, which he began as a publicist for Sammy Davis Jr. He then became a manager to Robin Williams, Billy Crystal, Paul Rodriguez, and many others. He's also a successful producer, and when I was first introduced to him, he was producing ESPN's sports awards show, *The Espys*. Though the show has now been running for a long time (and indeed, I would go on to write/consult/perform on ten *Espys*), this was only the fourth incarnation, and it was still a relatively unproven commodity. David hired me, along with my old friends Billy Martin (now Executive Producer of *Real Time with Bill Maher*,) and Jon Macks (longtime writer for Jay Leno) to write sports-oriented material for the host, Tony Danza.

Steinberg is a true character. Brash, friendly, irreverent, profane, but with a heart of gold. Truly old-school, in the best sense. He makes fun of everyone and everybody, which used to be okay in Hollywood. Now, because of the actions of people like Harvey Weinstein, Kevin Spacey et al, it seems like the pendulum has swung so far the other way that nobody can joke about *anything* without HR getting involved.

As for Mr. Steinberg, if you were looking to be offended, he'd make sure you didn't have to look too hard. He'd razz everyone and everything in sight, as would we all, and we thoroughly enjoyed it. Comedy writing rooms are not a place for the squeamish.

At one point, we were considering a joke regarding John Kruk's recent disclosure of successful testicular cancer surgery. I know, I wasn't quite on board even though Kruk himself said a lot of humorous things about the whole procedure. But I thought it would probably be best to let Kruk himself do that kind of joke if he so desired, rather than someone who was merely an outside party. But the best part of it all was listening to David speak to an understandably concerned ESPN executive about the joke. (David: "But we're not mocking the testicle that he lost, we're celebrating the one he still has!") The network understandably said, absolutely not. (Interestingly, years later when I worked with Lance Armstrong, who'd had the same surgery and was hosting the *Espys*, he eagerly did a joke I pitched: "Well, here I am hosting the *Espys*, live, in front of millions of people. I know you're thinking, that takes *ball!*" Of course, some humorless scolds masquerading as media critics took offense at this. We seem to be living in a time where even someone who has gone through a terrible experience is not permitted to make jokes about themselves. (We'll circle back, er, cycle, back to Lance later.)

The first *Espys* I wrote for was held at Radio City Music Hall in New York, so we all flew to Manhattan in February to spend two weeks preparing. As luck would have it, I had just decided to quit smoking a few days before we departed for The Big Apple. It was a lot easier to not smoke in California, where that habit was generally frowned upon. And as I mentioned earlier, smoking indoors had been largely legislated out of restaurants and office buildings by then. California of course has always been a health-minded state. The only thing that smokes in California these days are the trees, sadly. So I figured it would actually be helpful for me to be heading back to the cold east because I'd be a lot less tempted to step outside for a cigarette when the temperatures would be lower than an agent's scruples. However, at that time in the mid-90s, smoking indoors on the east coast was still very common, and I was mortified to find that at least half of the staff on the production smoked quite a bit on the job. Prior to this, my writing, especially under tight deadlines on live awards shows, was always done with a smoke or two. And now here I was, about three days off cigarettes, with everyone around me smoking like a grill filled with fatty ribs. But I figured if I could somehow survive this atmosphere for two weeks and not smoke at all, I'd be cigarette-free for good. Somehow I managed, and can happily say I haven't had a cigarette since.

Not that I wasn't tested in some unexpected ways, however. At that time, though I was working on some good projects, California is expensive, and I was basically living paycheck to paycheck. I was contracted to be paid after each week of working on the *Espys*, and somewhat surprisingly, I was actually paid on time on the first Friday I was in New York. I say "surprisingly" because it's a dirty Hollywood secret that getting paid in a timely fashion for many TV projects is a frustrating experience. If you're on a series that has a guarantee to be running for at least a year, it's a lot easier to get the paychecks on a consistent schedule, once you get that first one. However, the pre-production time and paperwork and other hoops that many business affairs departments put you through usually causes at least three weeks of delay before you finally start getting your paychecks in a steady and timely matter. As for "one-offs," it can often be weeks after you've already finished the show before you get paid, unless you really have your representation kick up a fuss about it. It's amazing how so many networks and studios expect you to turn in your work on time, yet they don't feel any obligation to pay you on time. Sad, but true, and still too common.

With all this in mind, I was delighted when I was handed a check after that first week, and since I was going to be in New York for several more weeks, I wanted to cash the check, so that I'd have spending money. Plus, I could then write out some money orders for bills I had waiting for me back in LA. (I stupidly hadn't brought my checkbook with me on the trip, and this was before online banking was really a thing.)

There was a Bank of America across the street from our hotel, and since I had a BOA account, that seemed a logical place to go. David Steinberg was looking to step out and get some fresh air, so he walked to the bank with me. As it turned out, it wasn't a full-service bank per se. In fact, I'm still not sure what it was. They had windows and tellers, but I'm not really sure why. I approached the first teller I saw, and explained that I was here working in New York, had an account with BOA in Los Angeles, and wanted to cash a check. As I showed her the check from ESPN, she eyed it suspiciously. I guess she wasn't a sports fan.

"Let me see your ATM card!" she ordered. I admitted I didn't have it with me. David shot me a bemused look.

"Do you have ID?" she barked gruffly. I produced my California Driver's License. She gave it a once or twice over, and handed it back to me.

"We can't cash this!" she announced. Which made me wonder, then why did you even ask for my ID? Just so you'd have a name to put with the face you're being rude to?

"Why not?" I asked.

"Well, it's not written on a Bank of America account."

"But I have a BOA account. Isn't that what matters?"

"No, this 'ESPN' needs to have an account with us as well." I knew I was definitely in trouble when she pronounced it "Ehspin" instead of E S P N.

At this point, David couldn't resist jumping in. "The check is from ESPN, the sports network. The Walt Disney Company just bought them a few weeks ago, massive deal, you might have heard?" She looked at him for a moment, then said "I don't care if Daffy Duck wrote the check, I'm not authorized to cash this."

"You mean Donald Duck," David offered unhelpfully. "Daffy is Warner Brothers."

"Listen, we're a branch, but we're not really a bank" she replied. I asked, "So, is there a Bank of America nearby that actually is a bank?" "Three blocks east" she barked, and seemed as happy as we were to have us leave.

As it turned out, the other BOA was a completely different story. Or, somewhat different. The manager there was at least friendly, and while she said they couldn't actually cash it right now, they could deposit it in my bank account, and the funds would be available the next day. That felt like a major win, so I deposited the check and David and I headed back to the hotel, all the while discussing how arbitrary banking rules seem to be. I've come to realize by now that there really is no set "policy" regarding anything with banks. It's purely based on what branch you happen to go to, what employees happen to be there at the time, and what their general mood is that particular day. Their only consistent policy is to be inconsistent.

My "victory" with the banking folks turned out to be quite short-lived. The next day I received a phone call informing me that the ESPN check had *bounced*. Seriously. Insufficient funds from the biggest sports network in the world. How could that be?

I went to David Steinberg and informed him of this latest development. He was sympathetic. (At least, I believe he'd have been sympathetic if only he'd been able to stop laughing.) "No, I'm sorry, Eddie," David sputtered between guffaws. "It's ridiculous, but honestly, only you would have this happen." "Well, I appreciate your anointing me as such a special person, but

I need to find out what is going on here!" I shot back. We marched directly to the ESPN accounting department.

There, we were informed there had been some sort of misstep while transferring funds from ABC, and many checks had bounced. (So much for me being special.) However, this was little comfort to me at the time. I'd been as polite as I could be for as long as I could be, but this (plus no cigarettes for over a week) had pushed me over the proverbial edge.

"This is unbelievable!" I shouted, causing people within a five-mile radius to stop in their tracks, as in that old E.F. Hutton commercial. "Does ESPN stand for 'Extremely Sloppy Payment Network?' You guys call yourselves the 'worldwide leaders!' Does that mean 'worldwide leaders in bouncing checks?' How can you bounce checks? What are you, club owners from Jersey? College kids who forgot to return the keg and put the deposit money in your frat account? I mean, I know you're now part of Disney, but I didn't realize that meant you'll be a 'Mickey Mouse' organization!"

A lot of silence, and blank stares later, one of the accountants piped up. "Sorry about that," he mumbled contritely. That suddenly snapped me out of my angry rant. I stood there, looking at everyone. It was as if I'd just come out of some trance to suddenly ask myself, Hmm, how did I end up naked on this bridge, wearing an explosive vest?" "I'm sorry, I know it's not your fault, it's corporate stuff," I sputtered. "But I need to have that money in my account, to cover checks I've already sent out. Don't want to bounce them, like some irresponsible....well, you know." They nodded, and assured me things would be corrected by the end of the day, and indeed they were. I tried to forget all about the whole bizarre experience, but Steinberg wouldn't let me. He still brings it up almost every time I see him, to this day. But then, David and I have quite a few ridiculous moments from the past that we enjoy reminiscing about.

During that very same week in New York, David entered his room at the hotel to find a puzzling memo left on his desk. It stated that he'd been called by a Mr. Jeff Rooasap, and asked that he return the call. "Rooasap? Who's Jeff Rooasap?" a genuinely perplexed David asked. The rest of us shrugged. Then, someone said, "Wait. There's a guy from ESPN named Jeff Rooey. Is that it maybe?" "Well, that's not really close," David muttered. "I don't know." After another minute of silence, the light bulb went on for everyone in the room: it wasn't "call Jeff Rooasap," it was, "call Jeff Rooey, ASAP!" Apparently the operator who took the call was not familiar with that term. We all burst out laughing, and David dialed the room phone. I figured he was calling Jeff back, but actually, he was calling the switchboard operator, to laughingly discuss what had happened. The guy David got ahold of wasn't the one who had left the message, but apologized for the confusion, in a very dry, professional way. But David wasn't satisfied. "No, no, I'm not looking for an apology. I just want you to admit that it's stupid and hilarious! Seriously, isn't that stupid and hilarious? Tell me that's not stupid and hilarious!" he chortled, over and over. David would not let the poor guy end the phone call until he relented that yes, it was indeed both stupid, and hilarious.

And yet, I can honestly say, it's not the most ridiculous case of butchering phone messages that I've been around. When I was working on a TV show in the late 90s — won't name the show or the person, don't want to embarrass them, nor do I want a lawsuit — we had a receptionist who took phone messages, jotted them down, then left them on our desks. This person was so astonishingly inaccurate with these messages that I began collecting my faves, and recently, I stumbled across this list of them…they are all 100% real…enjoy!

NAME AS WRITTEN ON MESSAGE	THE CORRECT NAME
Troy Applebee	Varol Ablak
Corny Elia	Cornelia
Your Son	Ahmos Hassan
Bob Dickman	Bob Nickman
Lisa	Lorie
Steve Areshim	Steve Archer
Chris	Bruce
Pritch Richmond	Bruce Richmond
Ellen Hasselhoff	Ellen Hoffstader
Joel Gowan	Joel Gallon
David Rainer	David Raether
Joy	Kelly
Eddie Feldmann	Kevin from Carolyn Strauss' office
Gary Levine	Jarrod Levine
Russ from the Improve	Ross from the Improv
Jeff Shinder	Jeff Schneider
The Assistant Pearl	Ross Perot
Laura	Elaine
Roger Parmer	Roger Paul

So...by comparison, maybe "Jeff Rooasap" isn't really that bad, right? But I digress. Back to the *Espys*....

I went on to write (and on a few occasions, perform) for ten *Espys* over the next thirteen years. Sadly, the first one was the last and only one with David Steinberg as Executive Producer. He was too busy with too many other things to helm any more of the shows.

* * * *

As an avid sports fan, I've generally enjoyed my *Espys* experiences, and it's great working with some fun people. Although, I've found the overall experience had a lot to do with the particular host of each show. The smoothest, and thus probably the most enjoyable shows were the ones hosted by Samuel L. Jackson. He is the very definition of the term "consummate pro." One year, I'd written a three-part sketch that we pre-taped to roll into the live show and make it seem as if it was happening in real time. The premise was that Joe Theismann really wanted to be a big part of the *Espys* and was pestering Samuel L. in an obnoxious manner, and Sam was blowing him off. I was a bit nervous when I first ran the idea by Theismann. You just never know who has a sense of humor about themselves, and who doesn't. At one point in the series of vignettes, Samuel goes into the men's room during the show and Joe is in there cleaning mirrors in a desperate effort to be involved. Fortunately, Theismann found it hilarious, and was a willing and eager participant.

Without thinking much about it, I'd written myself a small role in the sketches portraying the harried Executive Producer of the show, trying to keep the peace between Samuel and Joe. I've done this before in my career, where I'll write myself a small part in something, almost out of laziness of not wanting to go through further casting, then realize as the tape time approaches, oh yeah, I have to do some acting now.

There was a quick scene where I would walk into Samuel's dressing room playing the role of Executive Producer, and warn him about Theismann and his supposed machinations to be in the show. Of course, Samuel had okayed the scripts before we went to shoot them, but he was doing so many things that he hadn't focused on the scene that much. As we were getting ready to shoot that scene, he said, "Hey Ed, do you have a copy of the script for a minute?" and I handed him one. He looked it over quickly and said, "Great, ready to go when you are." And with that, we shot the scene in one take. He was flawless, and I realized, wow, he'd hardly had time to even look at the scene, and he was amazing! I was so glad that I didn't screw up. If we'd had to start doing multiple takes because of my mistake(s), I'm guessing I'd have gotten increasingly nervous, and it might have turned into a very uncomfortable debacle. But as I say, fortunately I'd studied my lines intently (even though there weren't many, but I was nervous!) So, one take it was! That's very rare, but that moment really showed me what a great actor is. The fact that with such little prep he could absolutely nail it in one try made me appreciate the true talent actors like Samuel possess. Very impressive.

My favorite work that involved Jackson was a short film we put together for the *Espys* one year. Several previously retired athletes were making comebacks that year, and the premise of the film was that Samuel L. used to play football, and had decided to make a comeback as well. However, in Samuel's case, he wanted to make a comeback in pee wee football, and play against little kids. So the film featured him dominating a bunch of ten-year-olds on the playing field, until ultimately a couple of the kids take him down, and he threatens to sue them for being mean. The entire thing was shot in the form of an *NFL Films* type of documentary, and we were able to get voiceover from the legendary Harry Kalas, (who'd taken over as the voice of *NFL Films* from the equally legendary John Facenda, the original "Voice of Doom.") Cleverly titled *The Comeback*, the film was a huge hit, and in fact won an award for Best Short at the Aspen Comedy Festival that year.

* * * *

There were many other hosts throughout the years, such as Tony Danza, and Matthew Perry. There was Jeff Foxworthy, Jamie Foxx, and other folks who actually didn't have "Fox" in any part of their last name. I mentioned Lance Armstrong before, and that was certainly an interesting experience. Armstrong had just won his record-shattering seventh Tour de France and I, like many if not most Americans, was giving him the benefit of the doubt regarding the rumors of steroid use. After all, he'd passed every drug test, right? But mostly, I believed him because well, I wanted to. A cancer survivor, a role model to millions. I just couldn't bring myself to think the worst. At least, not at that time in 2005.

The first time I met Lance was with the other writers and staff of the *Espys*, about a month before the show. He was renting a beautiful house right on the ocean in famed Malibu. Like so many nice places in LA, it is, of course, a pain in the ass to get to because of traffic. LA traffic is legendary, and for good reason. It's incredible. You become used to it, but it never seems to get any more tolerable. When I first moved there in 1994 it was pretty bad, but at least there were times during the day when it wasn't completely debilitating. Like many cities, it was bad in the morning, and bad in the early evening, the hilariously misnamed "rush hours." But you could find pockets of time where you could actually get from A to B (or A to C to B if there was a detour) and it wouldn't require bringing food rations along to survive the time period. But traffic has gotten noticeably worse, and sometime in the last ten years, those pockets of time seemed to have gotten sewn shut permanently.

The only thing more amazing than the sight of twelve lanes of traffic is the sight of twelve lanes of traffic *not moving*. Completely stopped. At one PM on a Wednesday. WTF?? I wondered how much time I had to put in as a resident before I too was eligible to start resenting folks from the east for moving here.

I remember riding in a taxi to the airport one morning at about five AM. Traffic was at least moving, but the roads were still absurdly busy. The cabbie asked me in exasperation, "Where is everyone going?!" I shrugged and said, "Usually everyone seems to be going exactly where I'm going at any given moment."

Friends of mine who have never experienced LA traffic always have a hard time understanding when they'd ask me, "How long is the drive from Pasadena to Burbank?" and I'd answer, "Anywhere from twenty minutes to an hour." But that's how it is.

As the years have gone by, and LA has somehow gotten more and more crowded, it's gotten to the point where I fully expect to endure a traffic jam even in my own driveway.

Traffic is always something one considers when living in LA, it's a necessary part of the calculation for everything one does. Which can make for some interesting internal conflicts at times. When I was working on the sitcom *Melissa & Joey*, part of my job was to go to the studio whenever we had a "run-through," that is, a rehearsal for the week's episode. Following the run-through, we'd convene in the writers room to discuss what changes we felt needed to be made, whether it was to cut some scenes, tweak others, or simply add some more jokes. Some run-throughs went smoother than others, and one could never know if we might be finished working in an hour, or five hours, or more.

One day, we went through the script following a very smooth run-through, and I glanced at the clock and saw it was three PM. I thought, "Wow, great, if I leave now, I'll be home in twenty-five minutes," just ahead of "rush hour." But then, I glanced at something in the script, and it started to percolate in my head that there might be an issue. Dammit. If I didn't care about my work and the people I was working with, I'd have kept my mouth shut and been out the door. But sadly for me, I do care about my work, and especially the folks on that particular show, so I did the professional thing and brought up my concern to the producers. This begat a big discussion, and we dug back into the script for a couple hours, just enough to ensure my drive home at six PM took almost 90 minutes. Oh, the price of integrity.

One of my worst traffic experiences was in 2017. I got a two-month job writing on a Netflix show that taped on the Sony lot in Culver City. The Sony lot is great, but it also happens to be the farthest studio from where I live. It was approximately 20 miles each way. Not really terrible. Unless of course, it's 20 miles of LA road, during rush hour. I'd leave my house every morning at 6 AM, and arrive at the studio at 8:15 AM. The return ride home would be about two hours, which suddenly felt like taking the Concord. Simply trimming fifteen minutes off the return at night felt like a real treat. Brutal. Normally, I'm able to avoid peak hours on the highway, but being unable to avoid it now, five days a week, made me realize why there were so many shootings on LA freeways. Despite everyone being stuck in the same boat, er, road, there were always people who would not let me into the lane I needed to get to, even when I'd put on my turn signal and give them a hopeful look. At best, they'd act like they didn't see me, and at worst, they'd look right at me and make sure I understood that I wasn't getting a break. It's like they're thinking, "Hey, I know we're not moving, but I still need to be in front of you."

So, my day consisted of four plus hours of commute, and ten hours of actual working time. I tried to explain to friends back east that it would be like living in Pittsburgh and driving to Cleveland to work each day, then driving home. The difference being, on the drive between Pennsylvania and Ohio, traffic would at least be moving.

To add to the pure joy of the experience at that time, I was dealing with an inflamed prostate. And I'm not talking about jerks who wouldn't let me into their lane, I mean an actual sore prostate. It was incredibly painful, and about the worst thing you could do with a sore prostate was… to sit in a car for hours at a time. It was like having a little Keebler elf in my pants who was using my testicles as a speedbag.

There were many nights I took a hotel room near the studio lot at my own expense in Culver City, because it just got to be too much. At that point, the show only had a commitment for one season, and we were shooting the entire thing over those three months. I started thinking, wow, what do I do if this show is picked up for another season? Move to Culver City? Rent an apartment here? That's not flippant, it's the actual calculations people go through when working out here.

As it turned out, the show wasn't picked up, and in fact, they screwed me out of my last week's pay. I know, I'm sure you're stunned to hear that some folks in Hollywood would be unethical like that. But that's another story and I'll circle back on that one later. (There's that phrase again, the one I learned from agents, i.e. "I'll circle back on that, I'll circle back..." More like circle jerk, but I'm way off track right now.) Sorry, how did we get from Lance Armstrong to traffic? Well, turned out Lance was trafficking in bullshit, so I guess that's my segue back...

Anyway, as the production staff met with Lance at his beachouse on that hot summer day in 2005, we were interrupted by a knock on the door from Lance's neighbor, who turned out to be Matthew McConaghey. Of course, it's a time worn tradition to have Hollywood actors portray the "wacky next-door neighbor," but only in LA is the wacky next-door neighbor in real life actually a Hollywood actor.

The ladies on staff — as well as some of the guys — literally swooned at the sight of the shirtless McConaghey asking Lance if he could borrow an axe. I wasn't sure which was odder: that Matthew didn't have his own axe, or that he assumed Lance had one.

At one point later that day, it was just Lance and me in the room. We were idly chatting, and I brought up the amazing fact that he'd just won his seventh Tour de France. I whistled in wonder, and asked, "Seriously, it's incredible. How did you do it?" He looked me in the eye and said, "Haven't you heard? I cheated!" He said it with no hint of a smile, but with some exasperation.

It was really an uncomfortable moment at the time, and in retrospect, it's downright chilling.

When Lance finally came forward and publicly admitted his guilt in 2013, I asked some friends, "Gee, should I be insulted that the one thing he still won't publicly admit to is having worked with me?"

Here's a few more stories involving folks I worked with on various ESPN shows:

ART DONOVAN & THE FABULOUS SPORTS BABE

Art Donovan was a defensive tackle for several NFL teams, most notably the Baltimore Colts, in the 1950s. Inducted into the Pro Football Hall of Fame in 1968, he'd since made a name for himself as an engaging storyteller, making regular appearances on talk shows like *Late Night with David Letterman*, as well as a myriad of programs on ESPN. He was known for his self-deprecating humor, most notably about his weight. He played at 300 pounds back when most of the league didn't even crack 200, and understandably, once he retired from sports, he didn't exactly worry about putting on any extra heft.

At the *ESPYs* in the mid-90s, I was tasked with putting together a short sketch featuring him and Nanci Donnellan, AKA "The Fabulous Sports Babe." She was one of the first female sports radio call-in hosts in the country, and was extremely popular. A plus-sized person herself, she was known for her fun, irascible style.

Her publicist came to me and one of the other writers days before the show and warned us, "Don't put anything about her weight in the script, okay?" I thought, well, fat-shaming isn't my usual source of humor, so no worries, but I said politely, "Of course. She's paired with the equally irreverent Art Donovan, so I'm sure we'll come up with a fun segment for them. They'll be great together."

So we helped Art and the Babe with some fun sports banter, and of course, Art kept ad-libbing jokes about his own weight that got big laughs in rehearsal, while the Babe stayed strictly with the sports angle of the script, as written. During a break, the Babe pulled me aside and said, "Listen, Ed, Art loves mocking his weight, but you might have noticed that I'm not a dainty person myself. Can't I get some jokes to make about my own weight?" Naturally, my first thought was, "Well, your publicist told us that would be forbidden!" but I simply answered, "Sure, okay." It's not like the publicist would admit to anything, anyway.

AL MICHAELS & JOHN MADDEN

Backstage at the *Espys* one night, I was chatting with announcing great Al Michaels and football legend John Madden as they got their makeup applied. I asked if they had any questions about their lines, or their marks on stage, but they were all set and ready to go. We made pleasant small talk, then they exited to the stage. The makeup woman turned to me and said, "They were so nice! Who are they?"

I was a bit taken aback for a moment.

"Well, um, Al Michaels is a legendary sports announcer," I sputtered, "Monday Night Football, the Olympics…you know, 'Do you believe in miracles?'"

"Yes, actually I do, but who is Al Michaels?" she replied.

"No, that was his famous call at the USA hockey upset in the 1980 Olympics. He's a very famous sports broadcaster."

"Oh, cool," she said. "I don't really follow sports."

"I guess not!" I teased her.

"What about the other guy?" she asked.

"He's John Madden. Hall of Fame football coach, broadcaster…"

She smiled and shrugged. I thought a second, then said, "Did you ever hear of the video game called *Madden NFL Football?*" She lit up instantly and blurted out, "Oh yeah, wow, that's him?! Cool!"

DICK VITALE

Everyone knows Dick Vitale for his ebullient style of broadcasting college basketball. *"He's awesome, baby! That kid's a PTP-er! A diaper dandy freshman! It's unbelievable, baby!"* These Vitale-isms have become part of the sports vernacular in America. The thing is, that enthusiasm is genuine, and not just for basketball, but regarding life in general. I fully realized this when, in the fall of 1995, O.J. Simpson was acquitted of murder charges in the famed criminal trial. The day the verdict was announced, I went into work at the Kodak Theater in Hollywood, where we were in the midst of prepping another *Espys* show. As I walked into the offices backstage, I ran right into Dick himself, who met me with, "Oh it's awful, baby! He murdered those poor people, it's unbelievable!" as if he was describing some terrible ref's call in a big game. It was like being stuck in some *Saturday Night Live* sketch, or some hack impressionist's routine. "What would it be like if Dick Vitale reacted to the O.J. verdict? I think it might go something like this…" All I could think was, holy cow, he's Dick Vitale *all the time.* That must be exhausting!

JACK NICKLAUS

Not to sound "too cool for school," but after working in the entertainment industry all these years, I've gotten somewhat immune to feeling any sense of being "star-struck." I certainly admire folks I've worked with (well, *most* of them), but as in any field, the more you do something, the more you take it all for granted. The only times I've truly been somewhat "star-struck" over the years is when meeting personal heroes, who may or may not be such a big deal to the rest of the general public. Meeting Jack Nicholson? Of course it's cool, but not nearly as big a deal for me as when I met world chess champion Garry Kasparov. I was able to chat easily with Nicholson since we were both working, but when I saw Kasparov in front of me, all I could do is stand there with a weird, shit-eating grin.

The other writers on the *Espy* staff were always amused at my "no big deal," wise-cracking attitude when meeting and working with the celebrities and athletes. Which is why it was extremely entertaining to them to see me suddenly reduced to the level of a nervous sixth-grader when I approached one of my sports heroes, Jack Nicklaus. Trying to be cool (after all, I was a Writer -Producer on the show), I walked up to him, stuck out my hand, and actually said: "Hi, Mr. Nicklaus. You're my biggest fan." He smiled and shook my hand as I realized in horror what I'd just said. "Oh, wow," I stammered. "I of course meant, I'm *your* biggest fan. Sheesh." He chuckled and said, "It's okay, I figured that's what you meant. Though I'm *your* biggest fan, too." I laughed, then asked him if he was good with the copy he'd be delivering that night, and he said he was all set. I did manage to recover some of my dignity, telling him about how my dad and I are both Ohio State alums and have followed his career closely. He was warm and appreciative, and it was a really nice interaction for me. But for the other writers, well, the moment was truly priceless, watching me reduced to a clumsy fan-boy. I deserved every bit of mockery they gave me for the rest of the show. (Incidentally, as I was standing next to Nicklaus watching the show on the monitors, one of the Joe Theismann segments was being played, and Jack stood there laughing hysterically. I somehow, barely, managed to stop myself from turning to him and saying, "Hey! I wrote that! That's my sketch!" I figured I'd already humiliated myself sufficiently by that time.)

I should mention here that I realize I'm lucky to have had such a good experience meeting someone I admire. As we all know, it doesn't always turn out that way. I try to give everyone the benefit of the doubt, you never know what's going on in someone's life at any given time. But the old saying, "Never meet your heroes" exists for a reason. I recall seeing one of the writers approaching track star Michael Johnson backstage and gushing to him, "Can I please have your autograph? It's the only one I really want to get!" and Johnson hastily signing a paper and exiting quickly (well, he is a track star, after all.) We looked down and saw that the paper the writer was left clutching contained nothing but some scribble that appeared to be something like the letter Z holding a balloon. Just totally illegible. And the writer said, "What the fuck is that? What a dick!" At least he has a nice story for future grandkids.

EDDIE GEORGE

I don't have many autographs from my adulthood, including Jack Nicklaus's. Nor do I have as many pictures as I'd like, honestly. But remember, a lot of my career was before the time when everybody carried a camera/phone/computer/substitute-for-any-quiet-self-reflection-ever device. I do have some nice photos that official photographers have shot at events, but even with smartphones being ubiquitous now, I'm rather hesitant to ask people I'm working with for photos. Hey, that's just me. It feels intrusive in a work setting. And I never ask for autographs. One, because I don't really collect them, and two, I feel it's unprofessional. However, handwritten notes from people like Billy Crystal, Marcia Gay Harden, Robin Williams, etc, are nice souvenirs that were freely given me, and I do appreciate those.

Also, Ohio State alums such as myself share a "Buckeye for life" bond that has sometimes caused me to violate the personal coda that I just mentioned. Though I didn't do it with Jack, I did invoke my "Hey, I'm a buckeye, too!" status to get a picture with Heisman Trophy winners Troy Smith and Eddie George. Having attended the same school always feels more like comradery than fan-boy type of behavior (or maybe I just tell myself that). The funny thing is, Eddie had just won the Heisman in 1995 and was there to accept an award at the *Espys*. And right about that time, some rumors had started circulating that he might have some sort of injury that was being kept quiet, and that it might hurt him in the upcoming NFL draft. All of that turned out to not be true, but I mention it because when I approached Eddie backstage, I initially said, "Hi Eddie, Ed Driscoll from ESPN." And his face fell instantly, and he looked nervous, and I realized immediately that he thought I was another sports reporter wanting to ask about these injury rumors. I quickly said, "I don't work for ESPN per se, just writing on the show here. I'm an OSU alum!" He instantly relaxed and flashed his million-watt smile. He was ultimately picked fourteenth overall that year (absurdly low, in my opinion) and had a terrific pro career.

Years later, I'd have another nice interaction with OSU QB Troy Smith who'd just won the Heisman, and luckily he never mistook me for a reporter. And that same year, I wrote some copy for OSU basketball star Greg Oden, who had led the Buckeyes to the NCAA Finals in 2007. He was an extremely gifted athlete, and only 19 years old at the time. So there was that strange dichotomy of this enormous guy, who spoke like a sweet kid. Of course, he was both. When I showed him the lines I'd written that we wanted to load into the prompter, he smiled and said, "Great, thanks." And I said, "Is there anything you'd like to add? Or take out?" And he smiled and said, "Uh, no, thanks." I nodded, then he shyly asked, "But you would change stuff if I wanted to?" I said, "Of course! Why, is there a change you'd like? Just let me know." And he said, "No, not at all. It's just really interesting to me. I thought people had to say whatever you wrote." "Oh, I wish!" I replied laughing. "Do people really want to change stuff sometimes?" he asked. I then regaled him with several stories of how people often not only want to "change stuff," but how incredibly rude they can be when "requesting" it. He was cracking up, and genuinely surprised by this revelation. It was so charming to see his lack of guile, and I thought, oh my, I hope he has good people around him when he gets to the pros, would hate to think sleazy people might take advantage of him. It's an all too familiar story, especially in professional sports. As it turns out, despite his incredible talent, Greg was not the luckiest person regarding injuries, another all too familiar story in sports. He'd had a severe wrist injury in college, but still played well enough to be the overall number one draft pick in 2007. This was followed by an even more severe knee injury early in his rookie season, as well as yet another knee injury two years later. Thus, despite his talent and hard work, he was never able to fully overcome his injuries. Sports, not unlike the entertainment industry, can be a very tough biz, that's for sure.

A few other *Espys* moments I witnessed/experienced:

- A Producer on the show "intercepting" cool jackets that host Matthew Perry had generously ordered for the writers, and instead keeping them for herself and her friends. (The people for whom the jackets were intended only found out about it years later.)

- Seeing Muhammed Ali emerge from rehearsals onto a side street in NYC and watching in amazement as a mob of people formed seemingly from nowhere and pushed and shoved each other trying to get autographs, as he did his best to comply. They absolutely swarmed him in a frightening, suffocating manner. I stood at a distance, feeling bad for him.

- One show where the host brought in his own writers, who proceeded to shout out joke pitches that everyone could hear *during the live broadcast*, as if we were all just hanging out and talking in a bar.

- Another host getting big laughs with his first three jokes, then messing up the fourth joke causing it to bomb, then blurting out, "I didn't write that!" Interesting that he didn't mention he hadn't written any of the jokes that went well, either.

- A Producer who took a great script and ruined it because they thought they were funnier than the writers and made a mess of what could have been a great moment in the show. I was so irritated that I "jokingly" threatened to give my VIP Pass for the private after-party the Producer was throwing later that night to the angriest, drunkest vagrant I could find in the street, but my conscience got the best of me and I figured, why add to the vagrant's miseries.

- When I went to talk to Bill Murray backstage to help him with his copy, he playfully asked, "Tell me Ed, are you the best writer here?" to which I answered, "Of course! Would they send anyone less to work with *you?*" He laughed and said, "Great point, Ed. Let's get to work!"

* * * *

While generally the *Espys* were well received by the public, there would be the occasional critic who decided to take us to task for whatever trivial matter they deemed worthy of throwing a public fit over. Such as the critic from the *New York Times* who took exception to Lance doing the "that takes ball" joke, because nobody should be joking about cancer, (even someone talking about their own experience with cancer, evidently.) This critic also complained about some stupid little joke that he also felt was not appropriate. After I read the review, I googled who this extremely sensitive person was, and he was listed as "*New York Times* obituary writer." Seriously. Who better to give notes and opinions on comedy than an obituary writer. He certainly wrote one for our show.

I actually penned a scorching reply, defending the network, the host, and everyone involved, and sent it to our show's Producers to read before I sent it to the critic. While they agreed with everything I wrote, they asked me not to send it, because it would just invite more headaches for all of us. I deferred to their wishes, but it's a sad example of how intimidated people can be by any over-sensitive malcontent with access to a keyboard. (And I mean the critic, not me.)

Speaking of sports awards, the coolest one I ever worked on was the 2005 *Laureus International Sports Awards*. As the name suggests, it's truly an international event, honoring athletes from around the globe. I got to rub elbows with people like Jim Rice, Anna Sorenstam, Roger Federer, Maria Sharapova, and David Beckham.

For me, it all began with a phone call from my agents saying that the show was looking for someone to write patter for that year's hosts, Morgan Freeman and Marcia Gay Harden. My name had come up, and they wondered if I'd be willing to meet with Morgan. Uh, yeah, I'm sure I can squeeze that in between my PlayStation sessions.

Marcia was away on a movie shoot, so I'd mostly be working with Morgan during the pre-production period, then we'd fly to the site of the show, Lisbon, Portugal, for the last week. In the meantime, Marcia would review her copy via email, give me her feedback, and we'd all connect in person at the theater.

When I first sat down with Morgan, it was hard not to be impressed. He was kind and friendly, but definitely had the aura of a cerebral and established artist. Our conversation began like this:

"Ed, I have to tell you something. I'm not funny."

I paused for a moment. Then I said, "Well, we're really in trouble, because I'm not funny, either!"

He looked aghast for a moment, then burst out laughing. "I know that's not true, Ed, but you had me for a second there."

"Yes, well, let's hope I'm kidding, but I'm pretty sure we can figure something out," I offered.

He talked about how he's known for his serious acting roles for the most part, not for comedy. And he was genuinely concerned that people would expect him to be funny in his hosting role, and he wasn't sure he could be. Plus, he was just coming off the release of *Billion Dollar Baby* (about as sad a movie as you'll ever see. Excellent, but sad.)

Then I had a thought: why don't we make that the hook for you? You'll play it as someone who just doesn't understand why people don't think you're funny. He warmed to the idea as I pitched that he sternly deliver lines like, "Why don't people think I'm funny?" while glaring into the camera. "Gravitas is *funny*, people. Did you see *Billion Dollar Baby*? Very funny! I don't understand this reputation I have!" That's how we handled the opening monologue for him, and of course, being Morgan Freeman, he absolutely nailed it.

Interestingly, the only time he didn't buy what I was selling was during a segment we shot that involved him riding along with some famous race car drivers as they went at breakneck speed around a track. I'd written a line that had Morgan exiting stone-faced from the vehicle, looking nonplussed, and when asked by a reporter how it went, he'd say something to effect of, "I think I bummed the drivers out by screaming like a schoolgirl." When Morgan saw the copy, he said, "Ed, I don't get it. I don't scream like a school-girl, you know?" "Yeah, I know, that's why it's funny, it's…ridiculous and…." I fumfered. After an awkward pause in which there was no reaction from him at all, I dropped the line faster than he'd been traveling in the race cars.

* * * *

The entire trip to Portugal was well, a trip. I'd been dating the woman who would eventually become my wife — and eventually, my ex-wife — for only a few months at the time of the gig, and for whatever reason, the Producers seemed eager to please me. So I asked if they could fly her with me to the gig, and sure enough, they did. It made for a fun time for her, but as for me, I had to work, and didn't have much time to spend with her. But she was happy to tour the city herself while I was in the studio. (We ended up going to some pretty glitzy parties at night, which honestly, if she hadn't wanted to go, I could have gladly skipped after working all day, but I was glad to take her.) We also went to a fashion show, walked a red carpet, and met the King of Spain. Seriously. I tried to tell her, "Listen, this isn't how my life is all the time, it really isn't!" but I don't think she believed me. (After we'd gotten married and a Writers Guild strike hit, I think she finally understood what I was trying to tell her earlier, and wasn't too happy about it.)

Overall though, Portugal was a great experience. Marcia Gay Harden was a delight to work with. I sent her an email after the event, thanking her for everything. I was completely taken aback when she sent a lovely, hand-written letter basically saying, "No, thank *you* ." Wow. First class actor, first class human.

On a side note, shortly after I got back from Portugal, my agent called with an offer from some live event to be held in Monaco. (This didn't help dissuade the "jet-setting" notion my soon-to-be wife had about my life and career, by the way.) They were looking for someone to write hosting material for popular tennis player/pinup girl Ana Kournikova. I'm sure it sounds snooty, but honestly, I just didn't feel like jumping on another international flight only hours after I'd landed home in LA. So I politely declined. I remember talking to my teenage nephews on the phone, and they were stunned and horrified with me. "You could be hanging out with Ana Kournikova right now!", they berated me. I tried to explain to them that it was actually work, and it's not like me and Ana would be making out and strolling along the shore, hand-in-hand, but it didn't assuage their incredulity. I also have to say, another reason for passing on the gig was that in the back of my mind I thought, "I'll have plenty of other opportunities like this in the future," which hasn't aged so well. That was in 2005 and I'm sorry to say, here in 2024 I still haven't been to Monaco, nor made out with Ana. But I'm really okay with both. Well, the former, anyway.

One of the most fortuitous things about connecting with David Steinberg at the *Espys* (besides all the silliness we both enjoyed) was being introduced to David's clients, Billy Crystal and Robin Williams. I was hired to write some material for them when they hosted *Comic Relief,* the show that raised funds to help those in need, particularly the homeless. Shortly thereafter, Billy was named to host the Oscars for what was then his eighth time, and he asked me to write with him on the show.

Billy was an old hand at this Oscar stuff, but I sure wasn't, and I was thrilled and nervous about the opportunity. (I won't even go into the details of how I got lost in a rainstorm the first night I was trying to find Billy's house, and how I was so full of nerves and coffee that I actually had to pee outside in one of the poshest parts of LA. I'm not hiding anything —nor did I that night, as it turned out— but I've already covered the story in detail in my previous book, *Spilled Gravy*. (Yep, once again, plugging another of my books within this book. How gauche.) But anyway, the day Billy hired me, I excitedly called my mom back in Pittsburgh, and told her the news. Here's how the conversation went:

"Mom, I'm working on the *Academy Awards* this year!"

"Well, that's nice, dear. Say, are you doing your laundry regularly?"

It's important to have a mom to keep one centered.

Eventually I was lucky enough to work on five *Academy Awards* that Billy hosted, and each one was a total blast. Our signature bit on all those shows was the short film that opened the telecast, wherein we'd superimpose Billy into various scenes from the "Best Film" nominees, and it was always a huge hit with audience and critics alike. What many folks don't realize is how difficult putting together those four-minute movies really was. Matching the shots from the actual movies so that it looked seamless required hours of setting up the lights, the costumes, adjusting green screens, etc. If you've ever been on the set of a movie, you know that it's kind of cool for the first 20 minutes or so, then the reality of just how tedious the process can be sets in. It can take an entire day to properly film one 30-second snippet. And since what we were doing was basically making a film, we had many long, time-consuming shoots.

Billy is one of the friendliest, most even-tempered people I've ever worked with, but he's also human, and these long days can put us all on edge at times. One evening, we were shooting a scene based on the movie *L.A. Confidential*, the iconic moment when Russell Crowe walks into a room and says, "Excuse me," and Kim Basinger, wearing a cape and hood, turns around to reveal her golden locks, hood, and glamourous looks. A beautiful shot. We were framing the shot so that initially, you only see the back of the hood and cape, but when the person turns around, it's not Basinger, but Billy, golden locks, hood, bright red lipstick and all. Billy shrugs and says to the camera, "Too much?"

Nearing the end of a typical 12-hour day, as we were trying to get this last shot ("the martini", as it's called,) right as Billy turned around, somebody off camera was carelessly fiddling with equipment, and we suddenly heard a loud bang as something metal hit the floor. Very frustrating, and nobody should have been doing anything during the actual filming, but there you had it. The director shouted "Cut!" and there was an uncomfortable silence. Billy's shoulders sank, and in a rare display of irritation, he addressed the crew. "Come on everybody!," he began. "I know these are long days, and we all want to get home to our families, me included! So, I'm going to take a five-minute break, and I suggest you all do the same, and let's come back out here and be professionals, and do our jobs, okay?!" And with that, he turned and strode purposefully to his dressing room.

The studio was very quiet, and after a few seconds, I trailed him into his dressing room. He looked at me and I said, "Um, you do realize that you just chewed everybody out while dressed as Kim Basinger, right?" Well, he'd forgotten that part, and when he looked into the mirror and saw himself, he laughed and said, "Oh, crap, no one's gonna take me seriously!" And I said, "Oh, but they did! And the fact they did is kudos to you! To get that kind of respect, wearing that bright lipstick, now, that is impressive!" We had a good laugh over the absurdity of it all.

The worry of ruining a take, or doing something embarrassing on set in front of a full crew, is always lurking. At least, it is for me. And with good reason. All kinds of goofy stuff happens, and it's quite funny, *especially if it's not you and you're observing it from a distance.* Once during a shoot that involved Tom Cruise, I was joking quietly with another writer about the crude topic of an "upper decker." If you don't know what that is, let me first say, I totally respect you. I didn't know what it was either until someone told me, and there's no delicate way to put it: it's when someone purposely poops in the upper tank of a toilet, causing anyone unfortunate enough to use it afterwards to see nothing but feces every time they flush said toilet for the foreseeable future. I always took it as a theoretical concept because I figured, hey, that's just one of those stupid things people say, nobody actually does it, right? That's my naïve hope, anyway, but I digress. The other writer had not heard of this phenomenon, and accused me of making it up. I was insulted yet flattered that he'd think it was my brainchild, and I said, "No, check the internet, I'm telling you, it's out there."

As it happened, he'd just gotten the latest iPhone, and was eager to show me its bells and whistles, though as it turns out, he'd hadn't actually figured those out yet himself. He pulled out the iPhone and whispered into it, "Hey Siri, what's an upper decker?" The phone did nothing. Perhaps it was as disgusted as a human should be about the entire thing. But suddenly, at an extremely loud volume which bellowed through the studio, Siri announced, *"Upper decker, vulgar, slang. The act of defecating —"* and as my friend desperately scrambled to turn the volume down, he accidentally made it louder. Now the entire stage had stopped what they were doing, to see what the commotion was.

Since this other writer was also a good friend of mine, I did what friends do in that situation: I dashed away from him as quickly as possible. He stood alone and desperately continued his attempt to silence Suri's pronouncement, *"—into the cistern of a toilet so that ensuing flushes result in a flow of feces..."*

He finally just shut the entire phone off and jammed it into his pocket, but it was far too late. Crew members were staring at him, and the final payoff came when Tom Cruise himself called out from the rehearsal area, "Who's talking about shitting into cisterns?" with a bemused chuckle. Naturally, nobody admitted to this, and Tom chuckled again, and went back to rehearsing. (I apologize for the scatological sidenote here, but hey, people talk shit. Sometimes, literally.)

* * * *

During the pre-production period, (the weeks leading up to the show), we always tried to keep jokes and other things we were working on from getting leaked in the press, to maximize the surprise and fun of the actual show once we went live. That's why our rehearsals for Billy's opening were always "closed" rehearsals. This meant that anyone who didn't actually need to be in the auditorium was asked to vacate, such as various ushers, production staff, agents, special guests, and anyone else not completely vital to our part of the show.

Now, "closed" rehearsal still meant probably 50 people involved, such as camera operators, floor managers, grips, sound engineers, lighting people, etc. That's not even including the writers, Director, and others in the production booth. But the fewer people there, the better chance we had to keep things amongst only ourselves.

One year, Billy and us writers were sitting in a conference room above the auditorium, preparing to go to the main stage to run through our material. Billy asked me to call down to the stage and tell them we were on our way, and to please clear the space of everyone besides us. I made the call, and we all started down through the labyrinth of hallways and backstage areas typical of grand theaters. I was walking next to Billy, chatting about something, when right as we got about 20 feet from the auditorium, a Production Assistant called my name out. I peeled off for a moment, collecting some papers from the assistant and having a quick chat about the next day's schedule. It was only about 30 seconds total, but in the meanwhile Billy and the rest of the writers had entered the auditorium, and I hustled to catch up to them. Right as I reached to open a door leading to the stage area, a burly security guard jumped in front of me. "Sorry," he said, "this rehearsal is closed. We just got a call."

"Um, yeah, I'm actually the one who called," I sputtered.

"What do you mean?" he said sternly.

"I mean, I'm the one who called to close the rehearsal. But, not close it to *me*. I'm one of Billy's writers," I said.

"Then how come you're not with him?" he inquired.

"I was, I was pulled away for a second, I was just about 20 paces behind him and the rest of the crew!" I replied in exasperation. I was now getting anxious as I could see through a window that the rehearsal was about to start.

"But it's a closed rehearsal," he said evenly. Well, he sure had his talking points down, I'll grant him that. But I could see this was getting me nowhere. At this point, I truly regretted not smuggling my Bowie knife into the building earlier.

"Listen, I need to be in there," I replied. "Please call Gil Cates, the Executive Producer, and tell him Billy's writer Ed Driscoll needs to get in there, immediately."

He continued to eye me suspiciously (I guess he thought the credential badge I was wearing around my neck containing my picture and the words "All Access" was something I'd sneakily crafted myself.) He eventually got through to Gil, who of course was inside, getting ready to start the closed rehearsal I had ordered on Billy's behalf. It was funny to hear Gil over the walkie-talkie, "What?? Why is Ed out *there*? Tell him to come in, we're about to rehearse, for God's sake!" The guard reluctantly opened the door, and when I walked in, Billy and Gil spotted me and said, "Ed, what in the world are you doing?" I didn't have the time or energy to explain the bizarre experience I'd just had, so I shook my head and shrugged, and they all laughed at me. They knew it was a story they'd hear later, unless of course I got barred from another area where I was actually supposed to be.

A word here about security guards in general. Look, I know it's not an easy job, and some of the folks that do it are really nice, and professional. But there's also a shockingly high percentage that you can tell are frustrated, wannabe cops, and perhaps frustrated, wannabe Putin's secret police. They give off the unmistakable vibe that boy, they wish they were armed, *then* they could show some of these show-biz types who's boss! I mean, I'm sorry the Secret Service rejected your application, but this doesn't seem like such a bad gig. Unless you want to make it one, I guess. So while you do hear legitimate complaints of celebs not being "friendly" with security personnel, I have also seen plenty of celebs being treated rudely by security. Of course, neither is acceptable. Here's a crazy thought: maybe *everyone* could treat *everyone* at least respectfully, if not kindly? Okay, I'll stop tilting at this windmill now.

A few days later, I felt a little better to see it wasn't just me that went through these experiences. It was mere hours before the live Oscars show, and Billy and I decided to take a walk around the back parking lot of the theater, just so he could relax and focus on his task ahead. As we stood off by ourselves chatting, a security guard suddenly approached and, noticing that Billy wasn't wearing his credentials, asked why he wasn't. (I always thought it a bit funny that Billy would ever need to wear credentials, but he did quite often while on set.) But since the show was starting in just a few hours, I guess Billy just didn't feel that an ID badge was a classy accessory to the tuxedo he was currently wearing.

I realized it was the guard just trying to be funny, which there's nothing wrong with, but I remember thinking, wow, maybe not the time to be doing some lame bit in a guy's face when he's prepping to appear in front of nearly a billion people on live television. Billy looked over at him with a smile, obviously thinking the guy was kidding, just like I did. But it soon became apparent this guy was totally serious, and he asked again for Billy to show his credentials.

As an awkward silence hung in the air, another guard nearby who had just seen this unfold quickly came over, nodded to me and Billy, and pulled the guard aside. We could hear him explaining to his colleague that no, this is the host of the show, he doesn't need to have any credentials right now, etc. And we could also hear the clueless guard defending himself, completely nonplussed, saying, "Hey, I don't know who he is, and it's a rule that everybody has their credentials showing at all times, no exceptions, blah blah blah," as his appalled comrade firmly pulled him further away from us and kept trying to explain things to him.

I looked at Billy and we both cracked up. "Yikes, what the hell?", I said. "Aw, he's just doing his job," Billy noted graciously. I nodded, and after a few seconds, Billy said, "But gosh, maybe he should pick up a newspaper once in a while, huh?"

Okay, I'm sure you're thinking, well of course there would be intense security surrounding an event like the Oscars. That was my thought too, until March, 2000. That's when, eight days before the *Academy Awards* telecast, thieves stole 55 Oscar statuettes. Not sure how they did it. Perhaps they slipped past while security was checking the credentials of the host.

Obviously, we had a field day writing jokes about the whole affair, though I can tell you, none of the Producers of the show found anything about the situation particularly funny. But hey, for us, lost gold was comedy gold, and we were happy with the material we prepared. Then, less than 24 hours before the ceremony, 52 of the missing golden fellas were found in a dumpster in an LA neighborhood by a guy named Wille Fulgear, and returned. The story was all over the news, and I got a call that night from the Academy, with a Producer saying excitedly, "Good news, they found the statues! Looks like you guys have a bunch more stuff to write now!" I feigned excitement, but honestly, we had so many good bits locked and loaded, ready to go, and it was deflating to hear we'd need to write a bunch more stuff in such a short time before the show.

I mean, I'm not lazy…okay, sometimes I am. But once we started throwing ideas around I enjoyed the process as usual. We added some material about the ones that were found, but also speculating about where the missing three statues could be. At one point during the show, Billy emerged from the wings holding a basket of oranges with an Oscar inside, saying, "Hey, look what I just bought from a guy near the freeway ramp!" A fun night as usual, especially for Mr. Fulgear, who got a seat of honor at the ceremony, with an on-air shoutout from Billy himself. And I'm sure Mr. Fulgear got past security a lot easier than I did.

Incidentally, three of those Oscar statues are still missing. So, poke around your attic when you have time, you never know…

* * * *

Let me tell you about everybody's favorite joke that never made the broadcast. This happened in 1997, the first Oscars show I did with Billy. First, some background:

In 1997, Bill Clinton was president, and this was several years before the whole Monica Lewinsky thing happened. But throughout his life, Clinton had been dogged with charges of sexual harassment. The most notable accusation up to this point had come from a woman named Paula Jones. She charged that back when Clinton was governor of Arkansas, he'd unwelcomely dropped his pants in front of her. (That behavior almost seems charming considering what he'd later be accused of. To Bill, he probably considered pulling down his pants to simply be "courtin'.")

On a different note, the most elegant, prestigious after-party following the Oscars is the Governors Ball. It's held immediately following the ceremony, in a ballroom in the same venue. Almost all the nominees make an appearance, where the winners can subtly carry around their statue ("Oh, this little thing??") and the runners-up can pretend to be excited for them, and drown their sorrows with food prepared by Wolfgang Puck. There's some pretty stellar entertainment as well, years I've been there the party music was provided by folks like Tony Bennett, Brian Setzer, Elvis, and the Beatles. (Okay, kidding about the last two, just wanted to see if you're paying attention.)

Billy has hosted the Oscars many times, second most in history only to Bob Hope. So, in the weeks before the show, I'd pitched a joke for Billy that really was just meant to make everyone in the room laugh, not considering it to be a serious candidate for the opening monologue. The joke was, "It's amazing, this is my eighth time hosting the Oscars. I've seen more Governors Balls than Paula Jones."

Everyone laughed, then to my surprise, Billy said, "Boy, that's hilarious. Let's put that in the script for now." I instantly felt a little nervous, thinking, I don't know, kind of a harsh joke, I don't want to bring us any trouble (as I already had a few times at the *Espys*.) The Writers Assistant dutifully placed it into the current monologue file, and we pushed forward. I wasn't overly concerned; we always start out with a huge number of potential jokes and the list gets whittled way down as we only have so much time in the broadcast. I figured it would be cut before it was even tried in rehearsal.

But as days, then weeks, went by, the joke stayed in the script, and before I realized it, it was among the final 20 or so jokes still technically being considered for air. At a closed rehearsal a few days before the show, Billy said it aloud onstage in front of the approximately 50 workers allowed in the auditorium. It was the first time it had been heard outside the writers room, and it got a huge laugh from the crew. Instantly, you could see the gears turning in Billy's head. As a performer myself, I understand the intoxication of a laugh like that, and realized, that would make it even tougher to cut. Billy stood on stage, looking out at us, shaking his head and chuckling. "Boy, I don't know, Ed. It's really funny, but I know Clinton personally, and I'm just not sure…" Suddenly, I was thrust into the odd position of trying to kill my own joke. The last thing I needed was to be the source of some public friction between Billy and the President of the United States.

"I totally understand, Billy, don't do anything that makes you uncomfortable," I began, "it's probably best if you don't—

"Let's keep it for now, please scroll to the next one," Billy advised the prompter operator.

At this point, I had totally mixed feelings. On the one hand, just like Billy, hearing that burst of laughter made me want to hear the joke in front of a packed house in a few days. But on the other, I had visions of him facing a shitstorm of bad publicity, and me never working in the business again. Hmm, I may have to make an earnest plea to Billy in private to remove it, I mused.

As it turned out, I never had to do that. At the last rehearsal the night before the show, Billy was making final cuts and said to me, as if it was breaking his heart, "Ed, I'm sorry. I just don't think I should do this one." "I agree, that's the best decision, for sure!" I blurted out, relieved. "Hey, it made us laugh, so the joke has served its purpose. It led a life well-lived." The other writers nodded solemnly in agreement.

End of the story? Well, not quite. A few days after the telecast, an item appeared in the media column of *The New York Times*. It read, "Here's the best joke we didn't hear at the Oscars. 'This is my eighth time hosting the Oscars. I've seen more Governor's Balls than Paula Jones!'"

Somehow, it had gotten leaked. Billy called and laughingly asked, "Did you see the *Times* ? You didn't leak that, did you?" "No, of course not," I answered. "Well, he replied, "that little joke just had a will of its own. It managed to sneak out there!"

*   *   *   *

Here's a side note about an odd yet fun tradition between Billy and me. One day, I walked into the Academy offices, and I don't know if it was my hair, or the way I was dressed, or whatever the reason, but Billy said, "Ed, you look like Lee Harvey Oswald." I replied, "I *am* Oswald!" then I quickly struck the famous iconic pose of Oswald holding his stomach and grimacing as Jack Ruby shot him. Somehow, this turned into a running gag, and anytime I'm working with Billy, he'll just randomly walk up and point his finger into my stomach like Ruby, and I strike the Oswald pose. I know, it's as crazy as it sounds, but always entertaining, what can I say?

A big part of the fun is seeing other people's surprised reactions whenever we do it in public. During one *Academy Awards,* we were standing behind the curtain, and right before Billy went out on stage, he suddenly whirled around and gave me the "gun," and I immediately struck the pose. He then calmly turned back around and strolled onstage to the applause, leaving me to stand there next to a stage manager and a security guard. They both gave me a puzzled look, then one asked, "Was that...Oswald and Ruby?" I nonchalantly said, "Yes, of course," as if it was the most ordinary thing in the world, then walked away.

After that particular show, I had a mockup of the famous Oswald/Ruby picture created that featured my face on Oswald's body, and Billy's on Ruby's. On the back I wrote, "Billy, you slay me!" He actually keeps it on his office wall to this day. It's always funny to hear from someone, "Hey, I had a meeting with Crystal today, and I saw you getting shot by him on the wall!"

Another interesting note about that particular Oscars. While I was writing on that year's show for Billy, I was simultaneously writing on a Warner Bros sitcom called *Nick Freno: Licensed Teacher*. The week after the show, Billy sent me a plaque he'd had manufactured that featured the television ratings for the past week as listed in the *LA Times*, and the top-rated show was the Oscars, and the *very lowest-rated show* was *Nick Freno*. Which means, amazingly, I actually wrote on both the highest-rated and the lowest-rated show in television, *in the same week*. I feel pretty safe in assuming that no one has ever done that in the history of Hollywood, nor is it ever likely to happen again. I mean, what are the odds of even having the opportunity to do so?

Being at the very top, and also being at the very bottom, at the same time. If that doesn't exemplify a career in the entertainment industry, I don't know what does.

*　*　*　*

While the Oscars show itself is what's most important for us writers of the program, it's often the "show behind the show" that keeps the staff truly entertained during what can sometimes be quite a grueling process.

One year, we had a Writers Assistant who, to put it kindly, marched to the beat of her own drum. And like a rogue drum, it kept the rest of the band decidedly off-rhythm. Generally, the role of a Writers Assistant is to be part stenographer, part organizer, and part sounding board. It's not an easy job. But then, neither is laying explosives for building construction. Which is why you hope that folks who aren't really able to do that job don't present themselves as competent in that field. The biggest problem wasn't that she made mistakes, which of course we all do. But she not only wouldn't admit those mistakes, she'd doggedly insist the mistake was actually *yours*.

It was like a bad game of "telephone." Someone would verbally lay out a joke or phrase exactly as we'd like it, and by the time it emerged from her computer, you didn't even recognize what language it was in. She'd confidently read it back, and when someone would gently say, "Um, that's not quite right," she'd accusingly insist that it's exactly as it had been said, so don't blame her.

(She'd have been a great court reporter. "No, your honor, he said he's *guilty*, he didn't say '*not guilty*.' You're wrong!")

Also, the number of typos, omissions, and misspellings was more comical than our jokes. Honestly, reading the documents after she'd printed them out was so confusing, the script may as well have been entirely redacted as if it were a highly classified CIA document. Her name was Shannon (though who knows, she might've gotten that wrong, too) and within hours of the first day of production, we realized we were in trouble.

Let me say, the folks in that writers room are nice people. Nobody wanted to argue with her, but during that first afternoon, we all exchanged plenty of surprised, bemused, and ultimately panicked glances. Even Steinberg, who as I've stated is not exactly a shrinking violet, was pretty much speechless. When we took our first break, after Shannon and a few others left the conference room, someone mournfully observed, "Oh my, she's not good."

Billy, who was too nice to pile on, simply stood up and silently wrote "Argh!" on the whiteboard and left the room. Well, it would be up to Steinberg to speak with her, or replace her, or whatever needed to happen. One of the joys of being in charge, right?

The day grinded on in a similar fashion, and we all did our best to do our work and not be too thrown by Shannon's eccentricities. We would typically come in and out of the conference room, retreating to our own offices to work on various things individually, then meet as a group to discuss, then back to offices, rinse and repeat.

In the early evening, I was in the conference room with a couple other writers, just the three of us, trying to hash out a segment. Steinberg entered, looking serious, and said, "Just want you to know, Shannon has gone home. So, if you need to have anything fucked up, you'll have to do it yourself."

Spectacular. Still one of the longest, hardest laughs I've ever experienced.

The next day, she was back, in all her glorious form. After another somewhat contentious session in the conference room, and documents more replete with typos than ever, we took a break. After Shannon exited, Steinberg said, "Well, this can't go on. I guess I have to fire her, though I'm not sure how to do it." I said, "Well, just send her a note saying, "You're FRIED." She'll understand that!"

Still one of Steinberg's favorite jokes of all time. As mentioned, it's nice when we can entertain ourselves behind the scenes.

A few other Oscars moments in passing:

- One year, Burt Bacharach was the musical director for the show. (For the record, I love the stuff he and Hal David have written over the years.) Billy and us writers were milling about backstage around lunchtime, waiting for our rehearsal slot, and we were all famished. For whatever reason, the food we'd ordered had still not been delivered, over an hour now, and besides being hungry, we were getting concerned that it would arrive when we had to rehearse, which meant we couldn't eat our lunch until dinner time. As rehearsal time approached, I suddenly started singing, quite loudly, *Where's our fucking lunch, Alfie?* Everybody cracked up, then I realized why there were actually laughing. Unbeknownst to me, Bacharach himself was about ten feet away from me, now wearing an amused expression. When I turned around and saw him, he said, "Oh, are those the correct lyrics? Wow, I've been singing it wrong for years!"

- As with most comedians and writers, ideas can and will pop into my head anywhere, anytime. I remember one lazy morning when I was lying on my bed in my underwear and an idea for one of the opening films we were making for the awards sprang into mind. I quickly grabbed the back of an envelope on the bedside table, scrawled the idea down, then went back to sleep. Weeks later, that idea was being viewed world-wide by nearly one billion people. I'd forgotten the precise moment when I conceived of the idea, but after the show someone asked me about it. "So were you just sitting in your office, hunched over the computer when you got that idea?" I blushed. "Not exactly," was all I could offer. Let's keep that our little secret, can we, reader?

- I found out the hard way that to write jokes about the nominated movies, it was really important to actually *see* them first. During one conference room session, I pitched a bunch of jokes about a movie I hadn't actually seen yet, and really didn't even know what it was about. Yet I came up with some caustic stuff anyway. After I read three or four of them aloud, to stony silence, I gave the other writers a quizzical look. "None of these are funny?" I asked incredulously. After a beat of silence, Billy said, "Ed, have you watched that movie yet?" I guiltily admitted that I hadn't. "Well, Billy continued, "it's about a bunch of children dying in a school bus accident. So I'm not seeing a lot of belly laughs available there." I nodded solemnly, and everyone cracked up. And thus, there were no *The Sweet Hereafter* jokes for us that year, or any year following, as far as I know.

* * * *

One of the cool things about working on the *Academy Awards* is they always give you a nice leather binder with your name emblazoned on it, to keep your script and notes in one place. One year, I went to the production desk to obtain my binder. I gave the guy my name, and he scanned his list, then frowned.

"I don't see an 'Ed Driscoll' here."

"Um, well, you see one in front of you. I'm one of Billy's writers. Can you check again, please?"

He scanned the list and frowned again.

"Nope. I do see 'Ed Divscoll.'"

"What?"

He handed me a binder that read, 'Ed Divscoll.'

I laughed. "Uh, that's *probably* me, but it should read 'Ed Driscoll.' "

"No," he stated adamantly. "This is how we have it here, it's 'Ed Divscoll'."

After a beat, I said, "Hey, are you single? There's a woman named Shannon I'd like to set you up with."

Now it was his turn to look baffled.

"Not a big deal, but I'd like a correct version of the binder, please," I continued.

"But that's how it's spelled!" he insisted.

I realized this was a hopeless conversation. "Well, thank you so much!" I blurted out. "Here I've been misspelling my own name all these years. I'm so embarrassed!" I grabbed the binder and left.

Naturally, when I showed the binder to Billy and company, they got an immense kick out of it, as well as my story about trying to set him up with Shannon. I eventually got a binder that had the odd name of "Ed Driscoll" emblazoned on it, and I truly cherish both keepsakes from that particular year. Naturally, the entire staff called me "Mr. Divscoll" for the rest of the gig.

Regarding my name, you might be quite surprised to find out how often it gets misspelled. And not just the easy-to-understand mistakes I've experienced, such as "Driscole" or "Driskell" or "Driscol." Setting aside the aforementioned Oscars binder incident, it's amazing how often people screw it up.

I'll never forget, when the publisher of my first book *Spilled Gravy* sent me a pre-publication copy, the envelope actually was addressed to "Ed Dricsol." In horror, I thought, oh no, what if they've spelled my name like that on the cover of the book! As I fearfully tore the envelope open, I was relieved to see my name was at least spelled correctly on the book itself. Another bullet dodged.

As I mentioned, some of the small mistakes regarding my last name are at least understandable. But what's really nuts is the fact that sometimes, even my *first* name gets screwed up. Seriously! It's two freaking letters! A couple of my favorite instances:

I'm a huge fan of the band REM, and I was beyond thrilled to meet Michael Stipe, the lead singer, at a book-signing event in LA. I introduced myself, we had a nice chat, he signed my book, and I left, trying to look cool even though I was as excited as a teenage groupie. I couldn't wait to race home and show the autograph to my then-wife. When I got home, I triumphantly flung the book open for her approval and together, we read aloud the words inscribed in the book: "*To Eb, best wishes always, Michael.*" We both cracked up, though her laughter was more sincere. (When I went to see REM in concert at the Hollywood Bowl a few days later, I was just waiting for Stipe to say, "This song goes out to Eb!", and pictured myself screaming, "It's *Ed! Ed!*" during the entire song.)

Another time, I had a meeting at a studio scheduled, and when I arrived I approached the receptionist and said, "Hi, I have a 1 PM meeting." She nodded, looked at her computer, and said, "Are you…De?"

"I'm sorry?"

"Are you De Driscoll?"

"Um, no. I'm *Ed* Driscoll. I think they switched the letters accidentally."

She looked at the computer again, then at me again.

"Your name isn't De?"

"*Nobody's* name is De!!," I blurted out in exasperation.

These stories are a source of constant amusement amongst my friends, who continue to this day to call me Eb, De, Ned, Mr. Divscoll, and everything else but my actual name.

* * * *

A few other memorable moments experienced on variety/sketch/talk shows feels apropos before I wrap this part up, so here goes:

The great David Letterman has always hilariously spoken of "show-biz weasels" and yep, I can confirm, they do indeed exist. One year, I was brought aboard a show that had already been on-air for a while, but was struggling a bit. They felt it wasn't as good as it could be, and they were getting a little panicked. As it turned out, the Executive Producer was an old friend of mine, and I could tell they had the elements to make the show a lot better, they just needed some fresh eyes and reorganization. There was a lot of good folks on the staff, and once I was able to run some interference for my friend by taking care of things he shouldn't have to be concerned with, the production really began hitting its stride.

Then, the network told us they were bringing in another guy as a "consultant." I had worked with this person on a show about a decade earlier. He had "credentials" that looked good on the surface, but those who had worked with him knew his real ability lies in sucking up to the right people, and being not the least bit shy to stab someone in the back if it suited his cause. I had seen that firsthand years earlier, but when I heard he was joining the show, I mostly shrugged and thought well, maybe the guy's changed, been a decade. (I know, I know. My lack of guile can be embarrassing).

I'll just call this consultant "Floyd," which is what we privately called him. (This was because he tended to mumble, like Floyd the barber on the old *Andy Griffith Show*.) Anyway, when I heard Floyd was coming aboard, my friend the EP called to ask me what I knew about him. And I said well, his reputation among fellow workers isn't great, but who knows, it may not mean anything bad necessarily. But I did warn the EP to be careful what he said around Floyd, because it would likely go right back to the network honchos. My guess was he was basically being added to the show to be a mole.

Floyd is kind of the classic "wolf in sheep's clothing," and his friendliness when he joined the staff was quite disarming. He had some good suggestions, and I thought, well good, maybe we can work with him. It was the final few weeks of the season by the time he came aboard, and I felt we had things running pretty smoothly at that point. There didn't seem to be much to worry about.

Of course, Floyd still exhibited signs of the questionable behavior I'd remembered. A classic moment occurred one day when me and the EP were trying to decide how to handle a particular sketch. We were trying to choose between what I'll call "Option A" or "Option B" as far as the direction of the piece. We hashed it out, and both agreed that option A seemed to have the best chance of success, so we prepared to load that version into the prompter for the afternoon's rehearsal that the network would be attending. Just then, Floyd ambled up to us, and when we told him we were going with option A, he became insistent that option B was better. He said that the network folks had seen both versions and believed in B much more. Now, the hierarchy was very nebulous at this point. Normally, the EP was the boss, and I was second in charge. But Floyd always had this passive-aggressive air of "you really should listen to me, the executives sent me here," so he often got the final say on things. We put option B in the script as he "suggested," and that's the version we ran for the afternoon rehearsal.

Following the rehearsal, we gathered backstage as usual with the network execs to get their notes regarding what they'd seen. The first thing the head suit said was, "Hey, regarding that one sketch…" (the one I mentioned above) "We felt it didn't work, wasn't there another version of that? We think that one would work better."

Now, if Floyd was any kind of secure, or even decent person, you'd think he'd say, "Well, I have to admit, these two guys wanted to go with that other version, but I talked them out of it, so that's on me. We'll put that other version back in." However, Floyd was neither secure nor decent, and as me and the EP sat there incredulously, he simply said "Yeah, that's a problem, I'll make sure we take a look at that." Not only not acknowledging his error, but basically implying that me and the EP had messed up, and Floyd hadn't caught it the first time, but he'd correct it this time.

Quite pathetic, seriously. But, in the world of bad showbiz behavior, it wasn't really a big deal, and we just laughed it off.

When the show ended its season, the EP was nice enough to take the entire staff out to a fancy dinner at an expensive place. It was a generous gesture, appreciated by all. Of course, Floyd showed up as well, and was happy to chow down on the EP's dime.

Hours after the dinner had wrapped, I got a call from the EP, who told me that he was just informed by the network that he was being replaced in his position for next season by, you guessed it, Floyd. A seriously stunning development, even in a business not really known for its humanity. As classless as the firing was, it was almost charming in comparison to the fact that Floyd had gleefully shown up to eat dinner paid for by a guy he knew he was about to replace.

Here's another fun addendum to that story: after the EP told me this, I of course felt sick, and figured well, I'm sure Floyd will replace a lot of people, probably including me. And hey, I didn't really want to work on a show where this was happening, and I told my friend that. But my contract was up for renewal for the following season, and I thought, this will be interesting to hear what the network has to say to my agents. Will they make an offer to keep me? Or will they just use the classic, "We're going in a different direction"? As I say, I had no intention of returning to the show the next season regardless, but I was morbidly curious to hear how the execs and Floyd would spin it.

Months went by, and I hadn't heard anything from the show. It's not unprecedented for the hiatus between seasons of a program to be pretty quiet, but it was still a bit surprising when my agents told me, "We haven't heard, we'll let you know when we do." And I said, "Okay, no big deal." Whenever anyone in the business asked about my future plans, I always demurred, not telling the story of what had happened with the EP. I figured it's his decision on whether he wants to talk about that or not, so I stayed mum.

One evening, my phone rang, and it was a good friend of mine, a brilliant writer and director.

"Hey, Ed! I hear your show is looking for a head writer!"

"Well, that's not good," I replied. *I'm* the head writer."

There was a pause, then he said, "Seriously? Oh man, I'm sorry, I didn't know what your position was, and I was gonna ask if you could put a word in for me. Yikes!"

I told him that I had been waiting for word of my future with the show, and I guess this was the word. I said, "You know, they'd be lucky to have you, and I'd be happy to give you an endorsement, but I'm suspecting it might not carry much clout at this point!" We cracked up, talking about how bizarre our business was. And that was it. That's how I found out they wouldn't be renewing my contract. No call from the execs, no call from Floyd, not even having the decency to say something like, "Hey, thanks for all your work, but we're gonna put our own folks in now," or something similar. I had to find out from a friend unknowingly applying for what apparently now was my *old* job. Truly my personal favorite "Hollywood firing" story ever.

Incidentally, weasels aren't just *in* show biz. They also tend to *surround* the industry. A quick story to illustrate: one day, after attending my usual 12 step meeting, I was chatting with someone I know — and who happens to be quite famous — as we were leaving the property. We split up and went to our cars, and right as I clicked on my key fob, I heard rustling in the bushes nearby. I immediately thought I was perhaps about to be mugged, so I held my keys out as if they were some kind of weapon. (Not sure what I thought I'd do with the keys, maybe wave them in the air in order to distract the would-be assailant? "Look! Shiny!") Thankfully, it wasn't a mugger. It was actually worse: it was a guy with a camera. My mood turned from one of fear to disgust. "Are you a paparazzo?" I asked him. He seemed stunned that I was even speaking to him, maybe he thought he was still camouflaged. Or maybe he was shocked that I knew the singular form of *paparazzi*. Either way, he answered in the affirmative.

Obviously, he'd been shooting pictures of the person I'd been talking to. I was enraged. "That person is just attending to a private matter. They're not walking a red carpet. Why are you taking their photo?" I demanded.

"It's my job!" he shot back.

"I understand needing a job, but there's a lot of other ways to make a living, you know." I lectured.

"Well, this is my job. What other job am I supposed to do?" he mumbled as he headed for his car.

"Perhaps one that doesn't involve having to hide in the bushes in order to do it?" I asked. But at that point he'd started up his car, and peeled out of sight.

I shook my head in disgust as I got into my car. How sad, I thought. But I hate to admit, my next thought was, "Wow, I wonder if I'll be in any of the photos he ends up selling? I could use the publicity!"

CHAPTER 2

Situation: Comical

Let's talk about sitcoms, shall we? When I first landed in Hollywood, I had the same thoughts that a lot of TV viewers have: why are there so many bad sitcoms on the air? Obviously, there's great ones, too, but I never could understand why so many seemed to be mediocre, at best. But once I got hired on my first sitcom, I began to understand the problem. The process itself is far more complicated than people realize, and also far more than is necessary, in my opinion. There's a lot of moving parts involved. As in any industry, the more people who have to "sign off" on things, the more products become diluted. Unsurprisingly, in Hollywood, there's no shortage of folks who feel compelled to weigh in on matters that they really don't understand. At best it's a nuisance, and at worst, it's fatal to the creativity of the project. And the source of most of these ruinous daggers is the phenomenon known as "executive notes."

Let me say right here, there are some great studio and network executives, whose input makes the shows better. I'm always delighted to receive any feedback that actually improves what us creatives are trying to do. In fact, the first executive I had experience with was Carolyn Strauss at HBO. She was secure enough to trust the writers' expertise on, you know, writing, and when she had a suggestion or comment, it was always helpful. Naively, this experience on my very first television show led me to the faulty assumption that all network execs would operate this way. Largely laissez-faire, and only weighing in when necessary. In fact, I couldn't understand why so many of the more experienced writers and producers I met seemed so disdainful of the execs. But once I started writing on sitcoms, I finally understood where the contempt was coming from.

How do these people even obtain their jobs in the first place? Well, often there's some nepotism involved. And we're often talking about someone who is fresh out of college, where they took a screenwriting class for one semester—and probably didn't get a very good grade—and now they're sporting their very first adult clothing, and are in the position of "covering" a show for their big bosses at the network.

As Kevin Rooney once acidly commented about these folks, "Weren't you like, getting donuts for everyone a couple months ago? And now you're running around like you're Faulkner or Hemmingway, telling experienced writers how to do their jobs?" Yes, Kevin. It's exactly what they're doing.

Sadly, most of these people don't understand the intricacies of the creative process, such as, when you make a change in Act One of a script, it has repercussions that ripple through Acts Two and Three. In a half hour or hour-long story, nothing occurs in a vacuum. I've seen execs pull at threads over and over, then be genuinely perplexed when the entire story unravels. I've always joked about clueless executives giving notes on the New Testament: "Why does Jesus have to wait three days to rise? Can't He just do it in one or two days, and we can save money on renting the tomb? Change that!"

I don't say all this with a sense of superiority. I just believe in allowing the people you hire to do specific things to actually *do those things*, without meddling. For instance, I know nothing about how car engines work. And that's why I take my car to an expert, who *does* know about these things. And I trust them to do what they think is best, and I check on the results. If there's still a problem with my car, I'll communicate with them and try to see why there's still an issue. What I *don't* do is stand behind the mechanic while they're working and make suggestions about what they're doing, while they're doing it. Wouldn't make sense, right?

And yet, so many executives feel they are writers themselves (which makes you wonder, then why don't you write, instead of merely criticizing others? Probably because you can't write.) I can't repair a car, or do plumbing, or lots of other things that I hire experts to do. And unlike some of these executives, I'm really quite comfortable admitting that I don't know how to do some things.

To emphasize again, unless someone is a complete egotist, helpful notes and comments are always welcome. We're all shooting for the same goal here, aren't we? That is, to make the project as good as it can be. Or at least, that *should* be our goal. But as we know from our childhoods on, not everyone plays well with others.

Having spoken with people in many different lines of work, I've come to realize that for whatever reason, writing is often seen as something that most everyone feels they can do, if they "put the time in." I have a friend who hires writers and animators for a major cybersecurity firm. He has said to me many times, in frustration, "When I post a job looking for an animator, there is usually only a small number of people who apply, because they have to have portfolios showing actual animation work they've done. But anytime I post looking for technical writers, I get thousands of applications, most of which have no real writing samples to offer. It's as if anyone who has ever written a blog, or sent an email, or a text, considers themselves a writer. It's frustrating to have to wade through all that."

Another friend of mine, a medical doctor, is married to a writer. One day he remarked to me that in general, people seemed to dismiss what his wife did, even though it took time and effort and talent. When I asked him what he thinks is the reason for that, he shrugged and said basically what my other friend had said: "Most people think they can write, and that it's not much of a 'real' skill."

Now, I'm not sure if it's really *most* people, but I do think *many* people feel that way. Listen, I don't want to discourage someone who might be a tremendous writer or comic or artist or singer or whatever, but just either hasn't taken their shot, or has never gotten a fair chance. Every year, I'm sent scripts from the latest sitcoms that have been greenlighted for production. And every year, many, if not most, of those scripts aren't nearly as good as ones that writer friends have created and sent me, seeking my opinion. My friends' scripts are often far superior, but because they don't have a particular actor attached, or a director everyone wants, or the latest online "influencer," the scripts aren't picked up by a network. Indeed, this has also happened with some of my own scripts that I felt were pretty good. None of us are immune to it.

There's no doubt there's an element of luck involved in all of it. Hey, life isn't a meritocracy, so it's truly absurd to think that the entertainment business would somehow be an exception.

I still vividly remember when my manager called me in my Vegas hotel room to tell me a network had passed on a series I'd pitched. The reason they gave? "Not original enough." I was flabbergasted. Please, tell me it sucks. Or you don't get it. Or it's too weird. Or too expensive. But please don't tell me, as I sit in front of a TV set currently airing no less than three syndicated "Judge" shows *at the same time*, that my idea "wasn't original enough!" There was, and still is, nothing on television like that "unoriginal" idea I'd pitched. And hey, maybe there's a good reason for that. But the "not original" critique was absurd. Yet the only thing surprising about hearing a ridiculous comment from an exec was that I somehow was *surprised* to hear a ridiculous comment from an exec. You'd think I'd be used to all this by now. Here's a fun sample of actual dialogue that occurred once between me and a studio executive:

Him: "I always describe your humor as 'clever.' "

Me: "Thanks!

Him: "People don't want 'clever'."

(UNCOMFORTABLE PAUSE, THEN:)

Me: "Um, thanks again."

Yet, I continue to be surprised by these things. That's truly on *me*.

I will always lament the fact that someone like say, Aimee Mann, whom I consider one of the greatest lyricists and songwriters ever, will never be as widely known as any of the Kardashians. That said, I'd much rather be *her* than *them*. She has a nice level of success, devoted fans, and her own artistic integrity. It's all any of us could ever shoot for in this business.

One last observation regarding all this. A few years ago, the brilliant screenwriter Aaron Sorkin gave an interview in which he basically said, just because someone calls themselves a writer, doesn't make them one, and that there's a reason people make a living screenwriting: they actually know how to do it. Somewhat understandably, his words created a pretty negative buzz from the general populace. It sounded dismissive, and elitist, and perhaps it was. But lots of professional writers were quietly happy he'd said it out loud.

I would never condescend to those who are working hard, writing great stuff, and just haven't gotten a break or two yet. But it's also important not to diminish those who have put in the blood, sweat, and keystrokes to do it for a living at the highest levels. Just my three cents in these times of inflation.

A side note regarding Sorkin: for years, he and I had the same literature agent. One day the agent said to me, "You know, you're my funniest client, Ed. But Aaron's my most successful client." Um, okay then. Back-handed compliment accepted, I guess, lol.

* * * *

I do understand that sometimes mid-level executives are in a tough spot. If a script seems to be working perfectly, they are nervous that they can't justify their paychecks. If they don't have any suggestions at all, what does that make them? My answer would be: secure and competent. There is much respect to be earned by following the old, "If it ain't broke, don't fix it!" axiom. But I also understand that these mid-level folks probably feel some undue pressure from their bosses to demonstrate that they are "contributing." And some of those upper-level execs can be quite clueless as well; not messing something up that's working just to put your "stamp" on it, is one of the best contributions someone can make.

I won't mention the bad executives by name because one, it's not nice, and two, it would take up the rest of the book. But I will name some of the excellent executives I've worked with, in no particular order: Carolyn Strauss, Tracy Pekosta, Tim McNeil, Robert Prinz, Phil Breman, Tim Johnson.

Truly, network notes are the bane of any showrunner's existence. Some of us handle it better than others. There's a legendary true tale of one showrunner who evidently was being driven slowly mad by the high volume of network interference. It all came to a head when the executives were having yet another session where they were barraging him with notes, and as they spoke he nodded continuously while scribbling furiously on his script, apparently making sure he was writing everything down. After the execs had finished their latest diatribe, they asked the showrunner if he'd gotten all that? The showrunner blurted out, "Look! A pony!" and showed them his script, where it turned out he'd been indeed sketching a drawing of a pony during the entire session. As you can imagine, he was "escorted" off the lot, probably by guys in white coats chasing him with giant butterfly nets.

In the late '90s, I was part of a fledgling show that a network had just greenlighted for production. It was a sitcom about two middle-aged individuals, each trying to find their way in their professional and personal lives, and the female lead's character was a single parent of a teenager. Now mind you, this is the show the network approved after buying the script, and shooting the pilot. All good. Except that, for whatever reason, from the very first week of the show, a swarm (or flock? Or herd? Or make-me-gaggle?) of network and studio executives descended upon our show and tore it apart like so much roadkill. It was a barrage of nonsensical, contradictory, mercurial notes, and within a few weeks, the show was completely unrecognizable from the show the network had supposedly purchased and greenlighted.

This led to chaos, which surprised only the executives. The rest of us were trying to explain to them that we needed to pick one direction, then all work together to row in that direction. Who knew that incoherent notes led to incoherent scripts which led to incoherent tapings which led to incoherent shows airing? Obviously I didn't take the screenwriting class the people giving the notes had been through in college, so how could I make educated guesses about any of this?

I was working with some great people on that show, many of whom are still friends to this day. But we were put in an entirely untenable position, and there was just no way there could be any good outcome to all of this.

The work of trying to jam square pegs into round holes, then when it finally fit, being told to make the pegs round and the holes square, made for a lot of very late nights. It became routine to work well into the wee hours of the morning. After one typically long, late night, we found ourselves trudging to our cars bleary-eyed at four a.m. We'd been there since eight a.m. the previous day, and the showrunner realized we had to have a little bit of a break at some point (he didn't want us to end up sketching ponies in the executives' faces.) So he said we didn't need to come in until 11 a.m. the next morning (which actually was *this* morning at this point.) Fortunately for me, I lived just a few miles from the studio, and I was able to zip home and get some sleep. When I pulled into the lot later that day at 11 a.m., the guard at the gate said to me, "Wow, you guys are lucky, banker's hours, huh?" I glanced about furtively, trying to determine whether I could actually strangle him to death and get away with it. But because there were security cameras everywhere, and that whole annoying "Thou shalt not kill" thing running through my head, I merely nodded and smiled. After all, he had no idea how late I'd been working, and I'm sure he's put in his share of long shifts. But, I will say, he is fortunate those security cameras were in place.

Another fun moment came a few evenings later, when I got a call while I was, of course, still in my office at the studio. It was my manager, who cheerfully told me he was at the Four Seasons Hotel in Hawaii, and guess who he ran into in the lobby? My agent! Isn't that cool?! All I could think was, wow, my representatives are in Hawaii, and I'm working til three a.m. every day for a show that will inevitably be cancelled. I am in the wrong part of this business!

After weeks of dealing with more bad notes than a kindergarten trumpet ensemble, the axe mercifully dropped, and we were cancelled after only airing three episodes. And who do you think got the blame for the show sucking and not working? (Hint: not the executives that caused the whole situation, I can tell you that much.)

On another sitcom I was working on, the network dictated that an episode of our show should be about the hazards of teenage drinking. The series was about a high school teacher, so at least it made some sense. As we were writing the script, the network got more and more determined to pound home the message that teenage drinking is bad! (Unless you're a teenager, presumably?)

As a result, the episode became steadily more preachy by the minute, like some sort of after-school special from the 70s. And the more preachy it got, the less funny it got. We kept trying to remind the execs of the "com" part of "sitcom," but they weren't that interested in the opinions of the people actually crafting the show. So, we plowed ahead, making changes to the script as they dictated, while also doing whatever we could to at least offer some humor along with the moralizing. At the end of an exhausting week, the night we were supposed to tape the show in front of a live audience, the execs unleashed one last arrow from their "wreck this episode" quiver. They decided that they wanted the star of our show to end the episode with a taped Public Service Announcement (PSA) about teenage drinking. You know, just in case someone didn't quite get the message in the *first twenty-nine minutes of the show.*

I was sent from the stage to the writers room to inform my fellow scribes that we were now tasked with writing up a PSA. They actually thought I was kidding until I finally convinced them that no, seriously, we have to do this. Then, mostly as a joke, I said, "Hey, how about this: we'll have our star say, 'As we've proven here tonight, there's *nothing* funny about teenage drinking.'"

We all laughed, then I got really intrigued by the possibilities. I mean, you could read that as just saying teenage drinking is serious, right? The more I thought about it, the more I realized, this is a perfect passive-aggressive line to try! So, I promised the other writers that I was going to take the line to the execs. I figured they probably won't notice how these words could so easily be interpreted as insulting, and we'll actually get the last laugh of having our star publicly confess on camera that this episode isn't funny!

I approached the executives backstage and earnestly handed them copies of the proposed PSA. They silently read for a moment. Then suddenly, you could see the lightbulb, dim as it was, pop up over their heads. "Wait," one finally said to me. "This sounds like you're saying tonight's show wasn't funny!"

I did my best shocked take. "What do you mean? Oh, yeah, right, yeah, I see what you're saying, sheesh, didn't notice…" I sputtered. Believe me, NFL defensive backs don't backpedal as fast as I did at that moment. "Okay, sorry, let me go back to the writers and we'll come up with better copy." I grabbed the papers back from them and headed to the writers room. My pronouncement that our pitch had been rejected was met with initial disappointment, then uproarious laughter that we'd even attempted it. We decided to count it as a win.

As we were writing up a new version of the PSA, we started discussing how in weeks past, sometimes the "suggestions" the execs had given us were indeed recorded on film, but ended up not making the final cut when the episode actually aired. And we hadn't heard a thing about that, no pushback whatsoever. Then, it dawned on us: *this group of note-givers aren't watching the show when it actually airs!* Hell, we could probably burn pictures of these executives on the air and we'd never hear about it!

So, after shooting all their "suggestions," including the PSA, we simply didn't include the parts we didn't like on the "final cut" (the version that was to be aired, and was sent to the execs to supposedly review before it aired.) And guess what? The episode turned out pretty good after all! It did demonstrate the dangers of underage drinking, but never lost its humor while doing so. A perfect irony: as the credited writer of the episode, I actually won an award from an alcohol and drug awareness group for accurate depiction of substance abuse issues. Little did they realize that the whole situation almost made me lose my own sobriety! (Kidding, though I can't speak for some of the other folks on our staff, ha.)

Okay, gonna give my feet a rest and get off the soapbox (for now.) But I will add, the bright spot regarding bad notes is that they do make me grateful for the sensible, helpful notes that occasionally come my way.

But speaking of PSAs…one of the most famous series of PSAs in existence is NBC's *The More You Know.* Which naturally makes it a ripe target for parodying, and we did just that on a Comedy Central show I worked on. It was fun to come up with twisted lines for various celebrities to earnestly say into the camera, such as "Talk to your kids about drugs. It's the only way they'll ever hook you up with the good stuff." We shot a bunch of them with Rob Lowe, who turned out to be just a terrific guy to work with. A pro's pro, he was taping a bunch of these mock-PSAs for us one day, delivering each line so sincerely that it was a task for the crew to not laugh until we'd cut after each performance. After he'd flawlessly read several bits into the camera, he was looking at the teleprompter at the next one we were going to do, and he started shaking his head, laughing, but simultaneously looking disgusted. "Oh man, this is sick! Did you write this, Ed?" I wasn't sure what the next one loaded in the prompter was, and said, "Uh, maybe, what is it?" He dutifully recited, "Make a lasting impression on a child's life. Kill yourself on a playground." The crew laughed and groaned simultaneously. "Um, yeah, sorry to say, that was me," I confessed. "Probably a little edgier than we're looking for. By all means, don't do any of these you're uncomfortable with, okay? We can skip it."

"Oh, no. I'm definitely doing it! But man, this is sick!" he said, laughing in spite of himself.

"Well, as you wish, Rob. Let's go for it," I answered.

And he looked sincerely into the camera, read the sick line, waited for the graphic and voiceover to say "The more you know…" and when I said "cut," he burst out laughing, as did the rest of the crew. "Man, that's just wrong, that is so terribly wrong," Rob kept saying as he shook his head and cracked up. Honestly, I couldn't disagree with him.

* * * *

MAKE ROOM FOR WRITERS

Let's talk a bit about the mysterious phenomenon known as — "the writers room." (CUE DRAMATIC MUSIC STING) *Dun Dun Duuuuuuuuh!*

It's oft-discussed but scarcely understood. Of course, there's the physical *room*, which generally consists of a conference table, chairs, computer, and white boards. Then there's *the room*. That's the magical place where much planning, creating, and outright scheming takes place — and that's just when choosing where to order lunch from.

Ideas, insults, even fists have been known to fly in this mercurial yet sacrosanct space. Personal stories are told, some funny, some not, all in the service of trying to come up with good stories and good dialogue for the show.

At various times it can feel like a therapist's office, a zoo, the floor of the stock exchange, a college party, or a wake. Or, a combination of all those things over the course of a full day. "Outsiders" might be somewhat shocked at the repartee that takes place there, but it's hard to explain to others that it's all part of the creative process. Which is why we all end up saying things in the room that we'd never say in the real world.

Spitballing ideas in writers rooms almost always involves blowing off steam, sometimes saying really twisted things, just to get a reaction. It's the kind of things people say at water coolers privately, but of course these days, everyone has to pretend they don't, or they could lose their jobs. But it's best to leave one's sensitivities at the door, so to speak. Hey, even I'm offended by stuff people say sometimes, but I would never question their right to say it. Besides helping us blow off steam, crazy, weird comments often lead to something we can actually use in the script. It's truly part of the creative process, like it or not.

Naturally, writing rooms differ from show to show, depending on the type of show, not to mention the type of personalities that are in charge of the show. But for the most part, Hollywood writers rooms are not for the squeamish or thin-skinned. At least, not on comedy shows. And at least, not on any of the *good* comedy shows.

In the 90s, and really right up until around 2015 or so, the writers room was a place where general rules of civility were gleefully suspended. Obviously, there are unacceptable behaviors that even writers rooms don't condone, such as physical violence. (Fortunately, I've never witnessed that, but I know writers who have.) And there was a show I worked on in the 90s where I felt some of the writers were inappropriately mean to others, and I thought well, if I was in charge of this room, I would not permit a guy saying, "I can't even begin to tell you how stupid that idea is!", when it was clear he wasn't kidding, just being cruel. But overall, I'm loathe to put any kind of repressive atmosphere in place in a writers room, because it unquestionably stifles creativity.

The tricky part of course is that almost everyone has their own defi-nition of what constitutes "inappropriate." And quite frankly, it's become fashionable for some writers to claim harassment or disrespect, only because the ideas they're pitching aren't being used in the show. Or, they didn't get a promotion they wanted. Or, any other reason folks can come up with. Again, there's some legitimate concerns out there, but in my opinion, the pendulum has swung too far these days.

The absurdity seemed to hit its nadir (at least, let's hope that's its nadir) in 2019, when well-known Sci-Fi and Crime Fiction writer Walter Mosley went public with his own story. Mosley was working in the writers room of *Star Trek: Discovery*, and told his colleagues of an incident where as a teen, he'd been hassled by police. He was vividly describing his harrowing experience, which he hoped might lead to a possible story for the show. The true story he told included him using the actual words the cops had yelled at him, one of which was the N word. Being Black himself, and telling a personal tale, Mosley felt no reason to refer to it as "the N word," he just repeated what the cop actually said to him. Nobody in the room objected to anything, the writers listened to the story and began kicking around ideas of how they might be able to use this incident in the episode they were currently writing. But the next morning, Mosley was summoned by HR, who told him one of the other writers had complained that he'd used the N word in the writers room. As you can imagine, Mosley was quite stunned, and explained that he was telling a story from his real life. But the HR person told the writer that the person who made the "complaint" would of course remain anonymous, and that Mosley had best not say anything like that in the room ever again.

So, let's review: an African-American man was telling a story he thought might be useful for the show, a story where he was called a racial slur by a law officer, and he's in trouble for doing so. If you don't think that's incredible and absurd, well, I'm not sure what to tell you. (But hopefully you kept the receipt for this book so you can return it now, because I'm sure you'll find plenty to be offended by in these pages.)

Mosley was so understandably disgusted that he quit the show on the spot, told his story to reporters, and has gone on to work successfully on many other shows. Shows where presumably he was not only permitted, but actually *encouraged* to speak of his personal experiences in an honest fashion. Imagine such a thing.

I guess this is as good a time as any to give my opinions on the rising censorship of comedy in general. I understand that generations change, and I think it's great that Gen Z is concerned about others' feelings, and being kind. We all should be. But I'm quite uncomfortable with the encroaching idea that laughing at ourselves, and others, needs to be overseen by an increasingly humorless "joke jury." On the one hand, it's nice that people want to be kind. But on the other hand, it seems like a lot of it isn't altruistic kindness but more of a smug self-righteousness.

It's ironic to me that back in the 1970s, the censorship came from the right, i.e. no jokes about religion, the flag, the country in general! And now, the censorship comes from the left, i.e. no jokes about sexuality, gender, people in general! To me, censorship of any kind is dangerous, no matter which end of the spectrum it comes from.

Going back as far as the Marx Brothers, or The Three Stooges, they didn't show up at the elegant dinner party and behave in a genteel way — they were boorish and inappropriate, and that's where the comedy came from. Some people today would rather have Mo, Curly and Larry show up at the banker's mansion, fix the plumbing perfectly, and politely be on their way. Now *that's* funny!

Gallows humor is how many people (such as, *me*) are able to cope with an often terrifying, out of control world. Comedians, and Jewish comics especially, still do more Hitler jokes than anyone I know. Is this insensitive? Is this because they see nothing wrong with what Nazis do? Of course not. Humor is the best coping mechanism ever given to mankind. It can take fear and the power of evil, and reduce it to a punchline.

I once posted a joke on twitter about a suicide bomber, and got a message from someone I didn't know, taking me to task about how bombers aren't funny, suicide isn't funny, and thus, none of what I wrote was appropriate. Instead of being defensive, or lashing out at this person, I calmly stated what I just told you in this book: dark humor is a tool that many humans use to navigate what can be a pretty dark world. Of course bombings aren't funny, suicide isn't funny, cancer isn't funny, on and on. But joking about them can take the sting out of these real-life occurrences that affect us all. Anybody who claims they've never made any jokes about tragic events at some point in time is simply not being truthful.

I ended my brief message to the offended party by adding, "I wish you peace." Which is true. I wish us *all* peace. We all just have different ways of pursuing it. To their credit, the person messaged me back saying, "Yeah, I get your point. Thanks, I wish you peace, too." Unfortunately, that kind of adult resolution is not too common these days. (I'm glad I was able to "defuse" the situation regarding the suicide bomber, so to speak. Oops, there I go again. I'm cancelling myself now, thanks.)

I do understand that when one does a dark joke in public, whether it be on stage or on the net, that one has to do their best to "feel the tone of the room." And anyone doing an edgy joke in public takes the risk of disapproval, and of course, disapproving is everyone's right as well. I have comic friends who do some routines that I actually do find offensive, and I'll even say that to them if they ask. But what's happened to Voltaire's concept of "I disagree with what you say, but I will defend to the death your right to say it"?

I remember having a conversation with a comedian friend of mine about a routine on religion he does, and he asked if I was offended. I said, honestly, as a person of faith, for sure it offends me. But as a comic, I said, it's funny, and well-presented, and thought-provoking. I never thought, wow, I don't like that, how dare he say things that make me uncomfortable! That shouldn't be allowed!

Netflix has the right idea: on-screen buttons read, "like this," "love this," "not for me." Notice there's no button reading "It's not right for me, and thus, it's not right for *anyone*, so take it down now or I'll march on your headquarters." Ironically, many of Netflix's employees marched on their own headquarters because of some jokes in a Dave Chappelle comedy special. (At least marching on one's own place of work is much easier, logistically.) I understand how folks can be genuinely outraged, but a lot of the protests in the last few years smell of faux outrage.

I'm sorry, but Richard Pryor's "white guys walking" bit is *hilarious*. But I guess I should be offended? Hard to know what to do these days. "Live and let laugh" is my credo. To me, comedy isn't about walking on eggshells. It's about stomping on the eggs to make an omelet. And whoever doesn't like the omelet, can simply choose a different meal.

Anyway, where were we? Oh yeah, talking about various shenanigans and tomfoolery in the writers room. As I mentioned, the chemistry of these rooms often varies from gig to gig. When I'm in charge of running the room, I try my best to encourage an atmosphere of fun, irreverence, and inclusion. I don't like people talking over one another, or rather, shouting, as happens sometimes.

There was one sitcom room I worked in where people constantly talked at once, yelling over each other, creating a din that was not exactly conducive to creativity. Me and a couple of the other writers found this very annoying. So to amuse ourselves, when everyone was shouting at once, we'd just start blurting out sounds. Not saying any actual words, just yelling gibberish as if we were sincerely trying to pitch some dialogue for the scene. It always cracked us up. And it *really* got funny on those rare occasions when the show-runner would suddenly make eye contact and say, "Okay, everyone, quiet down. Ed, can you repeat your pitch?" Then I'd have to make an actual pitch of some sort right on the spot, even though I'd basically just been making dolphin sounds.

(Another prank we writers like to play on each other occurs when one of us whispers something ridiculously inappropriate to another writer, just to make them laugh. Then that person will bust the other person, i.e. saying out loud to the showrunner, "Oh, that's good. Ed's got something, tell everyone what you said, Ed." Then there'd once again be that awkward moment where I'd have to actually pitch something that at least made sense, instead of the joke about the multi-pronged enema I'd whispered to my fellow scribe. It does keep one on their toes.)

* * * *

When I'm in charge of a writers room, I like to emphasize efficiency. That is, getting the work done during regular workday hours. A quaint notion, I realize, but it's been proven that folks can have fun and still get good work done in a timely fashion.

I've always contended than unless there's extenuating circumstances, (such as last-minute network notes, or a serious technical problem), that there's no reason for particularly late nights on most shows. I'd always heard that the *Frasier* staff worked "normal" 9-5 shifts, and their work seemed pretty damn good to me. Again, a lot involves the personalities and life-situations of those in charge. I've sat in rooms for hours at a time in the middle of the afternoon, not working, because the Executive Producer was out getting his haircut, and didn't want us doing any writing while he was away. Of course, this led to us all working through dinner and usually later, simply because we weren't making the smartest use of our time.

Some of the best-written shows I've been part of had a nice, humane schedule. And some of the worst shows I've been involved with had all kinds of crazy late nights, because of things like the EP having troubles with their spouse and they just don't want to go home. So, they basically keep everyone else hostage. And as you can imagine, a resentful staff rarely does its best work.

Some showrunners think it's a sign of dedication to their craft by constantly working until midnight, but I've always contended it's only a sign of disorganization. Working until three a.m. is not a badge of honor, in my book. Plus, I can tell you by experience that generally, no good work is being accomplished after ten straight hours at the conference table. Again, in the rare times there's an actual "emergency," such as a sudden illness, or a last-minute cancellation from a guest star, then by all means, the work has to be done as required. But to artificially inflate work hours because someone feels it shows "dedication" is total folly to me. In other words, get your haircut after work or on the weekend, like actual humans do, ya know?

The thing about sitcom writers rooms is, generally, you spend most of your day there. A writer is usually sent off to do a first draft by themselves, but then for the rest of the week, right up until the taping, that script is worked and re-worked in the room, by everyone on staff.

You have your own separate office to retreat to if needed, but 95% of the work happens as a group, often in ten- or twelve-hour shifts. As one writer described it, it's like being on a flight to London every day without actually being allowed to deplane and see London. I remember another frustrated scribe, during a particularly long day, complaining, "Hey, even prisoners get to walk around outside for an hour a day!"

Variety/talk shows tend to be more of a "hybrid" approach, which I certainly prefer. At *Dennis Miller Live,* we had meetings scheduled at specific times every day. But we all worked on material individually, on our own time, and all that mattered was that we had it ready for the appointed gatherings. So instead of everyone trying to write something together at once, we'd all come in with our individual scripts and ideas, then work on that as a group. I always liked the idea of setting my own schedule. Most of the writers tended to show up around ten a.m. As mentioned previously, I like getting in earlier than everyone else, maybe eight a.m. , so I can work with no distractions anywhere around me. I enjoy the calm before the storm. And I enjoy the storm, too. But at *Dennis Miller Live*, I'd generally have my work for the noon meeting already finished by the time the others came straggling in to start their day.

I'd then take a walk around the lot, or watch some baseball on the TV in my office, just catching my breath before the first meeting. Some, if not most, scribes seem to like to wait until the pressure of a deadline is right on top of them to start their work. But I've always been someone who prefers to plunge into my assignments immediately, and finish early rather than having it hang over my head.

In the last several years, mostly starting when Covid-19 hit, there have been writers rooms taking place via Zoom. It's not exactly ideal, especially if there's more than three or four people involved, but it works in a pinch. I'm guessing writers room Zoom calls differ from most business's Zoom meetings. One difference being, with comedy writers, people will actually *unmute* to make sure their peers can hear them burp after lunch. (I never said we were the most sophisticated lot.)

A little side story here: during the pandemic, I was hired by a corporation to write some humorous training videos, which was a nice little temp gig, especially considering all the productions in Hollywood had totally shut down. So, I just did my writing for them from home and emailed it in, and then I'd get some feedback, and do a rewrite if necessary.

At one point, one of the head honchos decided I needed to be in on some of the employee Zoom meetings, even though I really was just a side contractor. Why they asked me to be on these calls is something they're probably still asking themselves. But I thought, fine, whatever, they're paying me, I'll hop on some video calls, no problem.

At the first one I attended, the newly appointed CEO decided to have each person on the call introduce themselves and talk about what they'd done over their weekend. Seriously. I could tell he wasn't even remotely interested in the answers. He was merely interested in making his "underlings" do uncomfortable things at his command. I felt bad for the first few people who spoke, they were obviously ill at ease, not expecting this odd situation, first thing on a Monday morning. When it came to my turn, I blurted out, "Well, I spent the weekend talking to HR, because since I've been working with you folks, I've been mercilessly hazed as the new guy. In fact, last Friday they hung me up by my underwear on a hook in the locker room, and I had to call the fire department to help get me free. I won't name names here, but it's uncalled for, in my opinion."

To me, it was such a ridiculous statement, that I figured it might lighten the mood a little, you know? I mean, I didn't expect this to be a meeting like I was used to, a bunch of goofy, funny writers chatting. But I didn't expect it to feel like a police interrogation, either. My comment was met with stony silence, and in all the little video squares, I could see people's eyes popping out of their heads at what they'd just heard. After a long, awkward pause, the CEO said, "Well, I see you certainly have a bold sense of humor." And trust me, he wasn't saying it as a compliment. He abruptly called on the next person, and the meeting continued in its humorless slog. Of course, after it was over, I heard from a lot of employees telling me how funny that was, but clearly they were far too intimidated to openly display any amusement during the call. (Strangely, I was not asked to be on any future Zoom calls that didn't really apply directly to what I was doing.)

*   *   *   *

The writers room is not the only place where odd things happen during production. At one sitcom I worked on, an actress developed an odd habit of sometimes delivering her lines by twisting her mouth to the side, looking like Edward G. Robinson. This of course became a childish source of amusement among the staff. The director was constantly trying to get her to eliminate this little tic, but she seemed to like it, and was resistant to any direction otherwise. We all felt it was hurting the delivery of jokes, but again, she did not, so it was a constant battle. Anyway, one day, as a prank, I grabbed a fellow writer's copy of that day's script when he wasn't looking, and at the end of several of her lines, I scribbled, "Mahh, see? Mahh!", a la the aforementioned Mr. Robinson. Then I sneaked the script back onto his desk, figuring this will be fun once we get on set and he's surprised to read all those "mahhs."

Sure enough, during rehearsal, I was watching my friend out of the corner of my eye, and when he got to the first "Mahh", he started giggling, then looked over at me. I nodded proudly, and as the rehearsal went on, he laughed more and more. Of course, he did have plausible deniability about why he was laughing, he could just say, "Wow, these jokes we wrote are really funny!" I was very pleased with myself, that is, until a quick break during rehearsal, when he approached me and we were laughing at the silly stunt I'd pulled. Suddenly, the very actor we were mocking came over and asked my friend, "Hey, can I see your script for a minute? I just want to check my lines for the next scene."

We both went pale instantly. Obviously, the actors get their own copies of the script, and this was the first time I could *ever* remember one approaching a writer and asking to look at their copy. As we stood there silently, she gave us a quizzical look, then took the script from my friend's hand, glanced at a page quickly, then said, "Thanks," and walked away. Fortunately for us, she'd looked at one of the few pages where I hadn't scribbled "Mahh, see?" at the end of her lines. We realized we'd been spared quite a bit of embarrassment. That's what I get for doing stuff behind someone's back, right? As the old saying goes, if you can't say something nice about Edward G. Robinson, don't say anything at all…see? Mahh.

I can honestly say I never again wrote anything in anyone's stage script that I didn't want others to see. But can I honestly say I never engaged in other childish nonsense? I can say it, but not honestly.

From time to time, these hijinks have bitten me and fellow conspirators right in the ass, as we deserve. My friend and fellow comedy scribe Howie and I were once hired by an eccentric businessman in NYC to write a script for a short film he was producing. He had lots of silly, unhelpful notes, but we did our best to accommodate him. We did all this remotely, the client in NYC, and Howie and I at opposite ends of Los Angeles. The client would email us his latest thoughts on the script, and we'd make adjustments, and send the email back. Somewhere along the way, Howie and I thought it would be funny to email only ourselves a "response," one where we'd give our *real* opinions in a snide, obnoxious way. It was just a fantasy thing about what we'd like to send the client, but never would. So, while we addressed the client by name in these responses, we obviously only sent these "replies" to *each other,* making sure we left him off these fake rants, and only included him on the actual responses we wanted him to see. You might guess where this is going…

After cracking each other up for days with our "fantasy replies," I emailed Howie and wrote, "You know we're playing with fire here, right? Lol, one of these times we're gonna accidentally include him on one of these fake emails!" Seconds later, Howie sent me a reply reading, "Shit. I just did." At first I thought he was kidding, until I checked my inbox and saw that he'd indeed hit "reply all" on his latest snarky retort. I read what he'd written in response to the client's note: *"Your notes are embarrassing, Mr. X. Please leave the writing and humor to the professionals, okay?"*

Well. This was interesting. What would be the boss's response, and how would we handle it? About ten minutes later, we saw that Mr. X had sent a reply. With trepidation, I opened the email and saw that he'd responded, *"Listen, I'm sorry. I wasn't trying to hinder the process. But certainly, we can talk about this in a more civil tone."*

At that instant, Howie and I realized that our only play was to double down, and pretend we'd meant to send that inappropriate email. Howie wrote back, *"I apologize for not being more tactful, but we want to do the best job we can for you, and we feel it's best left to us to make some of the decisions regarding the comedy, and that if you'll trust us, you'll be happy with the end result."* Moments later he shot back, *"Yes, okay, fine. I do trust you guys."*

NICE SAVE!! And as an added bonus, he actually *did* leave us alone, and he was indeed very happy with what we ended up writing for him. Still, not the way I'd recommend dealing with somebody paying you good money to work for them.

*   *   *   *

Of course, I've also been on the receiving end of many pranks from my peers. One of the great things about having a free-flowing writers room where folks can speak their minds about anything, and tell tales of experiences they've had, is that it so often leads to a great story for a TV episode. I guarantee you, many of the craziest, funniest moments you've enjoyed on sitcoms actually happened to someone on the writing staff. It's often embellished and twisted into new directions, but the root incident that is the catalyst for the episode actually occurred.

I was working on a show for Warner Bros. with Carolyn Omine, renowned *Simpsons* writer, hilarious person, and all-around good egg. I was telling the entire writers room about the difficulties I was having with the accounting department, and how they kept asking me for the same informa-tion, which I'd repeatedly given to them, but I still hadn't received a check a month into the production. There was always some weird thing accounting blamed, from wrong address to wrong agency listed, to who knows what. (Perhaps some of the ESPN accountants were now working for Warner Bros?) My agitation in the writers room was good for many laughs among everyone, and we started discussing the possibility of a character on our show going through a similar experience with his employer.

When we took a brief break mid-afternoon, I went back to my office and was sifting through some papers when my phone rang. It was Warner Bros. accounting calling again. The woman asked for confirmation of my basic information, yet again. Full name, home address, etc. After politely reciting it all for her, she thanked me, then asked for my home address. I paused a moment, then said, "Didn't I just give you that? Okay, it's…" and as I was repeating it, she began laughing, then I heard a bunch of people laughing in the background. Okay, great, now they're all just laughing at me? Then the woman said, "Ed, it's Carolyn!" She was calling me from the writers room, just to see how far she could push me over the edge. "I can't believe how patient you were being," she laughed. "Well, what can I say?", I replied, "I just thought it was some really stupid person. I didn't realize that the stupid person on the call was actually *me*."

*   *   *   *

I am no stranger to embarrassing work incidents. When I was hired onto the series *Sabrina the Teenage Witch*, starring the wonderful Melissa Joan Hart, I was excited. A funny show, funny actors and writers, good stuff all around. I was actually hired by Melissa's mother Paula, who was an Executive Producer on the show, and like her daughter, a lovely person. Anyway, as you may or may not know, a "table read" in Hollywood involves the writers, actors, directors, and entire production staff having an out-loud reading of a script. It's where we all get to hear the script for the first time coming from the folks who will actually be saying the dialogue on camera. It's like a little radio play, I'd imagine, though I can honestly say I've never attended a radio play. Geez, I'm not *that* old.

It's obviously a vital and important step in the production process. At the first table read I attended for *Sabrina*, I was impressed at the sheer number of people gathered around the large tables (hence, "table read"). As the Director called us to order, a silence of anticipation descended upon the room. You could hear a pin drop. Well, you *could* have heard it, except that someone's cell phone went off, ringing loudly, over and over. We were all looking around, and I thought, oh man, I feel for whoever that poor sap is. Naturally, the poor sap turned out to be *me*, and to my horror, I realized the phone in my jacket, which I'd taken off and draped over a chair, was the one interrupting everything. I was stuck in that no man's land, thinking, well, hopefully it goes to voice mail very soon, right? Ugh, that's already five or more loud rings, it's gotta stop on its own, right? It would save me the humiliation of having to walk over to my jacket and turn it off in front of everyone. As it was, nobody but me knew where the disruption was coming from. But no, the phone had more rings than a thousand-year-old oak tree, and I had to slink over and silence it before we could begin. I mumbled some apologies, as all the other writers were giggling to themselves over what had just happened to "the new guy." I don't even bring my cell phone to table reads anymore, such was the trauma that I experienced that day.

The saddest part of the story? That cell phone moment would turn out to be only the *second* most embarrassing incident starring me on that show. Months after the "Who's the idiot that didn't silence their cell phone?" escapade, I was working in the *Sabrina* writers room when I suddenly began feeling queasy. (The cause later was revealed to be food poisoning from some seafood I'd eaten earlier.) In a matter of minutes, I was extremely dizzy and turning various shades of green. Another writer noticed and said, "What's up, Ed?" "My lunch!", I shouted, and dashed off to the bathroom. I was violently ill, as any of you who have had food poisoning can attest to. You feel like you're dying, and pretty much wish that you would. Anyway, after a very unpleasant interlude, I was able to clean myself up and emerge back into the writers room. Unfortunately, the bathroom was adjacent to where we were working, and studio office walls are notoriously thin. I had no choice at that point but to endure a barrage of ridicule from my peers, *"Was the scene really that bad, Ed?" "Looking over your own jokes again, Ed?"* etc. Hilarious, but brutal. In other words, the usual writers room experience. (Life hack: do not get sick then walk into a room of comedy writers. As I said before, sometimes you do wish you'd die.)

Occasionally, the noises heard near a writers room can be worse than even my little performance at *Sabrina*. One year, I was working on a sitcom starring Bob Saget, and while we were all taking a break in a little outdoor area on the roof of Paramount Studios, we heard what sounded like several gunshots. We looked out on the street, and seeing nothing particularly strange, we dismissed it as a car backfiring, and went back inside the conference room. Later that night, we all saw on the news a report of two men getting into an argument near the studios, and one apparently shot the other, right there by our offices. Nice. The next day at the office I said, "You know, when they said on the news 'there was a tragic shooting at Paramount last night', I originally thought they were talking about us filming our show!"

A few other magical moments from various sitcoms:

- Robert Townshend was shooting a sitcom on the stage next to ours, and for weeks we heard rumor of some crazy woman who was stalking him, and that all the guards on the lot were on high alert. (See? It's not just you, Vanna.) Sure enough, eventually they caught her. How? Well, during a taping of Robert's show in front of a live audience, someone noticed that the stalker was actually *one of the background actors in the party scene they were filming.* Proving once again, nothing gets past studio security. (Except for people who aren't supposed to get past studio security.)

- Adult film star —and of course, serious actress —Traci Lords was actually a guest star on a sitcom I was involved with. Unfortunately, she didn't go over too well, and the entire episode turned out to be a fiasco. I joked with my colleagues that our show was the only one she left off her resume due to shame. *"Hey, weren't you on that sitcom?"* *"Uh, no! You just recognize me from hardcore porn. Otherwise, I don't know what you're talking about!"*

- On another show, our guest director was Chet Forte, the legendary director of *Monday Night Football* during its halcyon years. The star of the show was giving everyone fits with their behavior for several days. Finally, Forte turned to us all and said, "That's the most arrogant person I've ever worked with in my life!", and stormed off the set. Whereupon I turned to the others and quipped, "Says the guy who worked with Howard Cosell for 25 years. High praise indeed!"

- Once, after we'd written some copy for actor Sean Connery, five of us spent the entire afternoon mimicking what we thought might be his response to what we'd sent him, in his trademark voice: *"What is dishh? I'm not saying dishh. Dishh is bulsshhit..."* Good times (timeshh).

- On my first day of work for one sitcom, I accidentally locked my keys in my car as soon as I pulled into the parking garage. When I tried to jimmy the door open, it set off the car alarm, which was louder than teenagers in a movie theater. I figured I'd call triple A and get some help, until I realized my phone was locked inside the car. I made my way into the studio and before I could even introduce myself, one of the security guards said, "Wow, what's with that car alarm? We'd better send someone up there to check it out." I told the guard that it was *my* vehicle making those wailing sounds currently reverberating off the garage walls, and he finally was able to get inside my car and put a stop to it. (Personally, I would have firebombed my car to avoid that embarrassment if I'd only had a Molotov cocktail handy.) I do know how to make an entrance. And all day, I overheard my new colleagues discussing that insanely loud car alarm that went off for 20 minutes this morning. I bravely chose not to admit any culpability whatsoever.

- I'm always amused with the never-ending attempts by writers to "sneak" dirty references into seemingly innocent things such as when we almost got a fictitious Italian restaurant named "Fella-Tio's" past the network censors.

- Generally, writing sitcoms is a collaborative process, as I've mentioned. Sometimes, actors ad-lib a line that works, and it stays in the final broadcast version. And sometimes, actors ad-lib a line that *doesn't* work, yet it also stays in the final cut! It's usually for political reasons — the star likes it, a studio exec likes it, etc. — even though it didn't really get laughs. Of course, that can be fixed in post-production by simply adding laughs that occurred elsewhere in the show to that particular moment. (It's what editors call, "sweetening.") Not a big deal normally, though sometimes, the timing of one of those jokes when it plays under opening credits can be unfortunate. On one episode of a sitcom, what I considered to be a bad joke was ad-libbed by the lead actor right at the beginning of the show. And *immediately* after the delivery on-screen of said clunker, a graphic appeared reading "Written by Ed Driscoll." Of course, that meant the entire episode, but to anyone watching, it almost seemed like that specific bad joke was written exclusively by yours truly. I could only laugh at the irony of it all, though still couldn't laugh at the joke itself.

* * * *

PICTURE THIS

While I've mostly worked in television, I've also worked on a few movies, too. *Inspector Gadget, Stuart Little, National Security,* and *Lizzie McGuire* are a few of the films I've been involved with.

I've done a lot of "uncredited" work on movies. Usually, I'm punching up the script by adding jokes and/or scenarios to make the film funnier. And sometimes, it's good that I'm not getting on-screen credit, based on some of the stuff I've contributed. Let's just say, I'm prouder of some lines more than others. Actually, I can give you an example of each from the same movie. I was brought in to add humor to *Scooby Doo* and *Scooby Doo 2: Monsters Unleashed.* I had a great time on both films, working with fun people.

In *Scooby: Monsters Unleashed,* the story begins with the Mystery Incorporated gang arriving at a red-carpet event. Fans of each character are shouting their affections, sporting t-shirts with the gang's likenesses, and waving adoring signs at their heroes. Fans call out, *"Daphne sign my shirt! Freddie, touch my ascot!"* And for Scooby, the script had some dogs barking at him, and we saw subtitles of what they were saying, reading *"Sign my bowl!" "Tug my chew toy!"* I flippantly pitched, "Let's have the last dog say, *"Sniff my butt!"* The writers laughed, and they put it in the script. I immediately felt a little silly, and made fun of myself saying, "Yep, that's my contribution: 'sniff my butt.' I'm a genius!" Everyone cracked up, and I said, "Well, hopefully I'll have some other lines that are a bit more highbrow." And one of the Producers said, "Well, you've set a pretty low bar there, Ed."

When the movie was close to being released, the producers and writers sneaked into a "test screening" of the film in LA. These are used to gauge the audience reactions to the film as it nears its final editing, and to give us a final chance to see what tweaks we may want to make.

We settled into some seats in the back of the public theater as the film began. Minutes into the movie, the dog yelling, "Sniff my butt!" appeared, and the entire theater roared with laughter. The rest of our crew laughed and pointed at me, mostly enjoying the fact that I was embarrassed about the line. I simply stood and deeply bowed to them, and sat back down. Several of the people sitting around us gave us weird looks, understandably. So, yeah, I shouldn't be such a joke snob, and in its context that joke was fine. But I was much more pleased with another line I'd written that appeared a bit later in the movie.

In this scene, as they approach an old house where they suspect a villain is living, the gang is captured because of a booby-trapped front door which results in whoever rings the bell being dropped into a cage below the property. When the gang winds up there, they discover that a lot of other innocents have been previously ensnared. The gang is shuffled past other cages where we see Girl Scouts selling cookies, and another cage with a door-to-door preacher, who asks them, "Have you heard the good news?"

And the line I pitched was Scooby answering, "Yeah, I've heard the good news. There's cookies!"

It's actually a line I liked, and it got a huge laugh in the test screening as well. Was it as big as the laugh for "sniff my butt?" Too close to call, honestly, but I guess the point is, both lines worked, so I'd done my job.

*　*　*　*

I was brought aboard another film one time, and when I entered the writers room for the first read-through, I plopped myself down at the long table filled with what I assumed were the other writers. People nodded hello, but there weren't any introductions. The atmosphere seemed a bit strained, but I've seen that before, so it didn't really throw me.

I noticed that each script on the table had our names on the cover, which wasn't unusual. What was a bit odd was to see large serial numbers stamped across every page of the script. This was apparently done to make sure there were no leaks of any kind of the script, and if any occurred, it could be easily traced back to the leaker. Now, believe me, I understand about protecting intellectual property, and I'm all for it. But considering what this particular movie was, a screwball comedy, I found this level of secrecy to be a bit over the top.

As I flipped through the pages, I turned to the guy next to me, assuming he was a fellow writer, and just wanting to break the ice, said, "Wow, kinda paranoid for them to have the scripts stamped. It's not like it's classified Pentagon documents, right?"

I didn't get the cynical laugh in return that I'd expected. The guy looked at me askance, then very seriously began to lecture me about how a major film such as this had to be protected, it's the smart thing to do, and on and on. I simply nodded and said, "Um, yeah, I see your point, I suppose." But it was an odd reaction when I was just being glib in an attempt to start a conversation with my fellow scribe.

Once the room had filled up and we were ready to begin, the guy I thought was a fellow writer turned out to be one of the Executive Producers of the film. So basically, I unknowingly had been ridiculing the seriousness of the entire project, right to the face of the guy who was responsible for all that seriousness in the first place. Who schmoozes better than me?

But I'm certainly not the only writer who's gotten embarrassed by some badly timed snarkiness. I was working with a writer friend on a movie that was actually far along in its production. Usually, I'm brought onto a project from the beginning, that is, before the filming of the initial script. But on some occasions, Producers will shoot the entire film, then when they look at what they have, they suddenly realize it's not enough. This is obviously a tougher situation for everyone involved, and often scenes can't be added, because all the actors and crew have been released from a project that should have been fully finished by now. Often, we end up writing lines that the performers will add via automated dialogue replacement, or ADR. It's the process of an actor dubbing new dialogue over scenes they've previously performed. Sometimes, the dialogue is added while the actor's back is to the camera since there's no footage of the person actually saying those words. It's a process my Writer-Director friend David Kendall calls, "Talking necks." Weird stuff, for sure.

On one such movie, the studio and Producers were in a total panic. The film was due to be released in less than a month, but still had major problems. They brought me and a writer friend of mine — let's call him Sam —in at the proverbial last minute to see if we could help. The first step was showing us the film as it currently was constructed in a private screening on the studio lot. Let's just say, it wasn't in great shape.

As Sam and I were walking back across the lot together to the production offices, he said to me, "Wow! There might not be any fixing that piece of shit!" Unbeknownst to us, the Executive Producer of the film was strolling along about five feet behind us and heard every word of this harsh, yet accurate critique. Sam spotted him seconds after his outburst, and they made awkward eye contact. "Yeah, that's why we hired you two geniuses to help," the EP said to Sam, without a smile.

So, we did the best we could, feeding lines into the talking necks under the intense pressure of having to release the movie at any minute. I swear, it sometimes felt like we were still pitching lines as they were loading the second reel of the film into various theaters' projectors, but we somehow made the deadline. And while it wasn't great, I can honestly say the film was better for me and Sam's efforts. So, the next time you hear a funny quip during a movie that comes from someone facing away from the camera, keep a kind thought for people like me.

CHAPTER 3
Meet Me at the Meeting

The entertainment business is big on "meetings". General meetings especially, where often times, studio heads will summon you to their offices. It's usually for one of two reasons: one, to prove to you that they can summon you, or two, to prove to *themselves* that they can summon you. And yeah, sometimes, it's actually so they can talk to you about your ideas, but that's much rarer.

With "general meetings", one can at least take some solace in the fact that the people you're meeting with *requested* to see you. (Though as you'll see shortly, that's no guarantee of a warm reception.) On the other hand, "pitch meetings", where you have to present and explain the show you're trying to sell, is usually much more daunting. My writer friend Jason Ward once told me of a pitch session he gave where he realized the executives were completely disinterested when he was only about ten minutes in. As he desperately tried to regain their attention, he found himself, as he described, "Sounding like an 8-year-old retelling a nightmare he'd had." *"And then...some aliens land...and then, turns out there's a ghost haunting the house...and, um...the one guy from the beginning I told you about actually comes down with an illness, and, uh..."*

Some general meetings turn out to be more fun than others. One time, my agent got me an appointment with Brad Hall, the former *Saturday Night Live* writer and performer, and husband of Julia Louis-Dreyfus. I hadn't met him before, but had heard only good things about him, and I was looking forward to it. So, I drove my car out to the Warner Bros. lot in Burbank.

Now, the studio lot is where the magic happens — especially in the accounting department. Somehow, TV shows and movies that generate hundreds of millions of dollars, according to Wall Street, are suddenly shown to somehow be *losing* money when it comes to sharing any profits with the creators, cast and crew that make these entities in the first place. But I digress.

Anyway, these lots are small cities unto themselves, truly bustling with activity, and it's why I've never liked driving my car through the lot. I much prefer to park off-lot and make my way on foot. I'm always afraid I'm going to back over a Hobbit by mistake, or end up being known as "That jerk who T-boned Betty White's moped." So usually, I ask my agent to request a parking space outside the lot, but inevitably I'm given a spot right outside the person's office, despite the request. The people scheduling the meeting are just trying to be nice, and it's actually flattering that they want to reserve prime parking spots for me. But as I say, it's hard enough to find specific offices on these lots as it is, without also having to worry about accidentally plowing over Jon Hamm in his golf cart. But that's my own neurosis, and my agent doesn't feel obligated to explain all that to everyone, and I never want to appear rude by turning a nice parking space down, so I just do as I'm told.

Sure enough, when I got onto the Warner Bros. lot, Brad's office was tucked away in an obscure, private area, and I was having a hell of a time finding the specific building. Then, just as I thought I was close, I turned down a street…directly onto a movie set that was filming. To my horror, I head the loud ringing of the bell indicating filming would stop, and heard the Director shout "Cut!" I was mortified, and as a Production Manager wearing a headset approached me, I was about to roll my window down and apologize for this ridiculous mistake I'd just made. However, unbeknownst to me, because I was dressed well, and happened to be driving a nice car, the crew assumed I was some self-important studio executive showing up to oversee the shoot. Before I could apologize, the production guy said, "Oh hi, sir, did you need to come down here and park by the trailers?" I hesitated a moment, and then, in my best arrogant, dismissive voice said, "Yes, I do.

Let's clear the way here, shall we?" I slowly drove down the street as people scrambled to move cameras and lights out of the way. A woman clutching a clipboard motioned to a space reserved for the studio execs. But instead of parking, I merely looked at the space, nodded and kept on driving, until I was gone. In my rearview mirror, I could see puzzled and angry people trying to figure out what had just happened. Did some idiot just drive through our movie set? I wasn't about to stick around to answer that question.

A couple minutes later, I found Brad's offices, and saw a space with my name on it, and pulled in, still glancing furtively about to see if any of the people from the film crew had followed me. I seemed to be in the clear, and I dashed into the building. The receptionist said, "Oh hi, you must be Mr. Driscoll. Any trouble finding us?" "Not at all," I shot back, as my series of lies continued.

When I got in to meet with Brad, I couldn't resist telling him what had just happened, and he howled with laughter. At first he thought I was making it up until I convinced him that no, sadly, it was all true. He turned out to be a great guy, and we had a really fun and fruitful discussion. As I was leaving, he said, "Hey Ed, do you want me to give you a lift? Or are you gonna crash a few more sets?" "No, thanks, I'm gonna drive myself," I laughingly replied. "I actually need to earn some more Screen Actors Guild credits. I think I have a new career making unintentional cameo appearances."

*　*　*　*

I'm a big chess enthusiast. I love to play, ever since I was a kid. I follow the pro circuit. It's a beautiful game. And as a member of the US Chess Federation, I receive their monthly magazine called *Chess Life*. It's obviously a pretty niche publication, but one I always enjoy reading. And also, one that most people don't even realize exists.

One afternoon I went to a meeting about working on a sitcom, and as I was waiting to meet with the Producer, I noticed that pinned on the bulletin board behind his desk was a copy of the magazine, *Chess Life*. I thought, awesome, a fellow chess fan, and I was genuinely excited to talk with someone who had my nerdy interests.

When the Producer came in and we shook hands, I said, "Hey, I couldn't help but notice *Chess Life* up there!" He cackled and said, "Oh my God, I know, right?! It's an actual magazine, seriously! One of our writers saw it at the newsstand and had to bring it to us. Hilarious, right?!" Recovering quickly, I sputtered, "Oh, yeah, I mean, how sad, yet funny. That's a real magazine? *Chess Life?* That's an oxymoron, right? Ha ha!"

He laughed, and we went right into discussing his show. Note: to my fellow chess geeks, I'm truly sorry I sold you out there, but I just didn't have the nerve to defend us in that situation.

(This reminds me of when I brought a girlfriend with me to Las Vegas where I was attending the International Chess Festival and yes, it's a real thing. After we checked into our room, we wandered down to the ballroom where the various events would take place, and as she surveyed everyone chattering excitedly, she turned to me and said, "Oh my, this isn't going to be nerdy, is it?" "It's a fucking *chess festival!* I mean, what do you think?", I shot back, laughing.)

But, there are some meetings where I'm actually more embarrassed for the person meeting me than I am for myself. My agent once set up an interview for me with the people running the show *America's Funniest Home Videos.* A pretty basic, but pretty entertaining, franchise. At one time, it was hosted by Bob Saget, but at the time of my meeting, it was hosted by Tom Bergeron. Tom is a great guy, a terrific broadcaster, funny and amiable, onstage and off. I'd worked with him previously when I filled in for a friend of mine who wrote for *Dancing with The Stars* but had a gig elsewhere and asked me to step in for a bit.

A side note: the weeks I was working with Tom coincided with the time I had been dating the woman who'd eventually become my wife—then my ex-wife (which is generally the order). I had only been dating her for about four months, and I was thinking of proposing, but really wasn't sure that was smart, considering the short amount of time we'd been together. One day backstage I was talking to Tom about my conundrum, and he said, "Well, my wife and I were only dating about a month when I proposed, and we've been married for 25 years." Now, we all know stories about people who dated for years, then got married, and broke up shortly thereafter. And there are other stories, such as Tom's, where people got married very early in their courtship, and it lasted forever. I found Tom's story inspiring, so I took the plunge. And I'm happy to say, I've forgiven Tom (mostly).

At any rate, when I found out I was meeting with folks regarding a show he hosted, I told Tom and of course, being the extremely gracious person he is, he said, "Great, I'll put a call in to the producers and give you my highest recommendation." I certainly appreciated that.

While this sort of gesture would normally work heavily in one's favor, in this instance, the people running the show were also the writers. And evidently, they weren't too happy about the suggestion from the network that the show could use some new blood. I didn't realize all this before I met with them, but it quickly became clear during the meeting.

I was ushered into the office of the two men in charge, and I was my normal, friendly self. I began things by remarking how fun it must be to work on their show, getting to write so many jokes. After all, it was a simple yet can't-miss formula, funny clips and funny quips from the host.

However, they scoffed at my lack of knowledge. One of them haughtily intoned, "Oh, no, this is a *lot* more complicated than you would understand. It's not just about jokes. It's about nuance, and pacing. It's a very special skillset."

I didn't say it aloud, but all I could think was, "Oh my God, guys, this isn't Shakespeare. It's *Funniest Home Videos*! Why are you speaking about it in reverent tones as if it's the fifth gospel of the New Testament? It's basically clips of guys getting hit in the balls on camera. Get over yourselves, will ya?"

But, mostly out of respect for Tom, I merely nodded as they described how difficult their work is, in a tone that made it imminently clear that I was not in their league. A very odd experience.

I was polite, and left feeling somewhat confused by it all. As it turned out, those guys were apparently able to convince the network that no, there certainly wasn't any "fresh blood" needed, and even if so, there's certainly nobody else out there but themselves who are capable of this demanding and important work.

Believe me, I'm sympathetic to my fellow scribes. Writers are often treated pretty dismissively by executives as they're "climbing the show-biz ladder", then when they finally get put in charge of things, the perceived power quickly goes to their heads. It's not an excuse, but it is a bit of an explanation. Fortunately, it's a small minority of people entrusted to oversee shows who can't quite seem to handle it, but they are out there.

Another prime example of this was a meeting I had with a guy I'll call Richie. I had not met him before, but he'd just had his pilot script picked up to go to series, and was now putting a staff together. It's an exciting time for any showrunner, because the odds of a script even getting shot as a pilot, let alone greenlighted to go to series, are very small. And of course, there are no guarantees that a show will go past one season, or even complete its first season. Such is the nature of the beast.

My agent sent word that Richie wanted to meet with me, which is usually a sign that the person seeking the meeting likes your work and wants to gauge in person if you'd be a good fit for the show. Meetings are usually a great way to close deals for me because people considering hiring me see that I'm friendly and funny and not an asshole. (My agent always says, 'You're a great closer, Ed!" to which I jokingly reply, "So why are you getting a commission if *I'm* the closer?") Meetings with potential employers are also a chance for me to make sure that they, too, are friendly, funny, and not assholes. It's important for both sides.

I suspected things were "off" when I first arrived at Richie's office. Even the waiting area was very dimly it, and the receptionist looked rather grim. I was kept waiting longer than usual, but wasn't too concerned about it. Eventually, the receptionist ushered me into another room that somehow was even darker than the rest of the office. Seated behind a big desk was Richie, with stacks of scripts scattered across his desk. The entire place had the feel of an interrogation room at some CIA black site. Richie exuded an aura of importance as if he was single-handedly keeping the free world safe. He pointed for me to have a seat, then shook his head and gestured to all the paper on his desk. "This is all I do anymore, read potential staffers' scripts," he intoned mournfully, as if looking through obituaries.

"But exciting to get a new show on the air, right?" I offered hopefully.

"It's a lot of work," he grumbled.

Which of course I knew, having been in his position before myself. He sifted through the papers and pulled out my resume. Gotta say, I've never had someone I was meeting with pull my resume out in front of me, but hey, everyone has a different system. He looked at the paper, then at me. "So, you write for Billy Crystal, huh?" he said, in an oddly skeptical tone.

"Um, yes, I do a lot of work with him. Great guy."

"So, if I called him, he'd say he definitely knows you, and works with you?"

I sat in stunned silence. This was bizarre. I don't know, did he have a lot of people sent from agencies who put things on their resumes that aren't true? And he certainly knew of me by reputation, which again, is why *he* was the one who'd requested to meet with *me*. I hadn't asked for any of it. Was he thinking I'd nervously blurt, "Oh, wow, you mean, you're going to check with the names and shows listed on my resume?? Dang, didn't expect that, please don't!! And let me scratch off that part that lists me as a two-time Super Bowl MVP!"

After an awkward silence, I said, "Yes, of course. Do you want me to try him on my cell right now?"

He waved his hand dismissively. "Nah, that's okay. Listen, I gotta look at a lot of scripts, lots of people want to work on this show."

"Well, I wish you the best of luck," I said, and saw myself out of his office.

On my drive home, I called my agent and recounted the weird experience, and he seemed as taken aback as I was. "Huh, that is strange. Don't worry, I'll look into it," he told me. "It's really okay," I replied, "It was kind of funny in a sad, Hollywood way, and honestly, I'm not too eager to get involved with this guy. I'm kind of hoping he's not interested in me, either!" We laughed and said our goodbyes.

As it turned out, Richie didn't offer me a job on his show. And it also turned out that his show was a complete bomb, and was pulled off the air after only two episodes. It was a very high-profile flop, and despite the uncomfortable nature of our meeting, I actually felt kind of bad for Richie.

About six months later, I was asked to be a Creative Consultant for a hit show on ABC, and on my first day there, I was greeted on the set by none other than Richie. At least, I think it was him, but this guy was all smiles and handshakes. "Hey, great to see you, Ed!" he enthused. The show's Executive Producer said, "Oh, do you guys know each other?" Before I could even answer, Richie said, "Oh yeah, and I'm a big fan of Ed's. Have you read his book? It's great!"

I paused for a moment, wanting to say, "Wow, I met a guy a few months back that looked *exactly* like you, but that couldn't have been you, 'cuz that guy was a jerk!" But I didn't say that, and I instead was friendly, just like I'd been at that bizarre first meeting we'd had months earlier. I guess Richie had really gotten quite a slice of humble pie after the cancellation of his show, and was now actually lower-ranked on the staff of this program than I was. I felt no sense of Schadenfreude, just sardonic amusement. I made no reference to anything unpleasant from before. I simply said, "Nice to be working with you," and smiled.

But there is a lesson in there. Instead of talking down to me when you "outranked" me, then kissing up to me when I "outranked" you, maybe just…treat everyone equally, with respect, no matter what your work positions are? A novel concept in Hollywood, but I really do think it can work. I dare to dream…

* * * *

One of the most interesting — and surreal —meetings I ever had was with the legendary and revered late-night television Producer Peter LaSally. He was the Executive Producer of the *Tonight Show with Johnny Carson*, the *Late Show with David Letterman*, *Late Night with David Letterman*. 90 years old, and still in the game. A few years back, he took over *Late Night with Craig Kilbourne*. Craig was originally an ESPN anchor, then became host of his own show at CBS.

My agent Richard called one day and informed me that Peter had just taken over as EP on Kilbourne's show, and that they were looking for a new Head Writer, and he'd like to meet with me. I was excited. As I say, LaSally is a true showbiz icon. "Hey, you've seen the show, right, Ed?" Richard asked. "Um, well, actually, I haven't." Richard couldn't hide his disgust. "Ed! Every time I set you up with a meeting, you haven't seen the show! You gotta watch more TV!" I said, "Well, where were you when I was growing up and my mom was always saying, 'You watch too much TV!' Wait til I tell her that apparently now, I don't watch *enough* TV!" I promised him I of course would look at a few of the episodes on YouTube, and I'd be familiar with it all by the time of the meeting.

Believe me, I was well aware of the dangers of not having seen a show before meeting with those in charge. I was told a classic story by the afore-mentioned Kevin Rooney. Kevin had once had a meeting with a show that he'd never seen before, and was having a nice chat with the Executive Producer. Kevin feigned as though he was familiar with the show, and successfully charmed his way through the meeting. As they were wrapping up, the EP mentioned the name of an actress that knew Kevin, and heard they were meeting today, and wanted to send along her regards. Rooney's eyes lit up, and he said, "Oh, I love her! She's the best. Please tell her hello when you see her. What's she up to these days?" The EP gave him a confused look, then said, "She's one of the stars of our show." Kevin then did his best to act as if he had been kidding, but it was evident that he seriously didn't know she was one of the show's leads, and he awkwardly showed himself out.

Ever since hearing that cautionary tale, I've always made sure to watch several episodes of whatever show I'm interviewing for. And as I watched the Kilbourne program, I was pretty underwhelmed. I didn't think the show was good, and I didn't think he was particularly good as a host. Well, I'll just be courteous at the meeting, I thought, but I definitely can see why they need some help.

When I was escorted into his office at CBS, I found LaSally to be friendly, but somewhat brusque and intimidating. Seemed about right for someone with his extensive background. Very "old school". He got right to the point.

"Well Ed, I really love the stuff of yours I've seen," he began, "and I hear great things from people who have worked with you in the past."

"I really appreciate that."

"So, tell me what you think about Craig, and the show."

I took a breath. I wanted to be truthful, but respectful. "Honestly, I think any show can always get a little funnier. And I think Craig is um, a smart guy, but——-

"Well, you're wrong!" he interjected. "Because he's an idiot."

"What's that?" I stammered.

"He's not smart at all," he continued. "That's why I need somebody like you to tell him, hey, look, *this* is funny. Do *this* stuff, this is what's funny! Can you do that for me, Ed?"

I simply nodded.

"Okay then. It was nice to meet you, and your agent will hear back from us soon."

We stood and shook hands, and that was it. I can truthfully say, I've never been to a meeting—before or since—where the Executive Producer told me, as a potential hire, that the host is an idiot. At least, not *before* I was officially hired on their show.

I ended up not getting the gig after all, which I was kind of fine with. I really had just wanted to meet LaSally, and I got an interesting story out of it, without actually having to work under his supervision. Probably best for both of us. I could only imagine what he'd say about me in future meetings if we hadn't gotten along.

* * * *

While some meetings leave one wanting, others can result in way more than was expected. Here's a case in point.

A few years ago, I did a show at the Improv in LA, and a very successful Executive Producer named David Hoberman was in attendance. After the show, he approached me and said some kind words about my set, which I of course appreciated. He got talking to my manager for a while, who later told me, "David is developing a new television show, and he'd like you to come to his office to talk about it." I assumed he was looking for someone to write the pilot episode, or punch up the pilot episode, or something like that.

I was happy to go meet with him, and did so a few days later at his digs on a studio lot. Now, David is your classic idea of what a big-time Executive Producer is, right out of central casting. A big, handsome, confident guy, very smart, friendly but kind of intimidating. He started describing a show he was co-creating with screenwriter Andy Breckman. It was amazing to hear him say that the lead character, a hypochondria-riddled, self-doubting detective, was actually based on David himself. He told of how he'd grown up with OCD, and was a major germaphobe as a young adult. I told him I found that surprising, considering the seemingly well-adjusted person who sat in front of me. He smiled and said, "Well, we're in the illusion business, right Ed?"

A really good dude. I was enjoying chatting with him, and thought he'd be fun to work with, for sure. The project sounded really smart and interesting, actually more of a drama than a comedy, but as is the case with many of the best dramas, David wanted it to be infused with moments of intelligent, dark humor.

I completely understood his vision, and I finally said, "Really sounds great. So, what writing role are you considering me for? Helping with jokes? Or maybe, coming up with funny scenarios for the pilot?"

He said, "Well, actually, I was thinking of you for an on-screen role."

"Oh, wow, yeah, that's nice," I said. "So what, does the protagonist have a funny neighbor or fast-quipping friend you have me in mind for?"

"No, actually, I was thinking for the lead."

Wha? "Well, geez, I'm really flattered, but this is a drama, and I'm not a real actor, you know?" I demurred.

My mind flashed back to an incident from my days in Boston, just prior to moving to the west coast. I don't consider myself a classic "actor," (nor does anyone who's ever seen me act). I know how to bring my own comedic personality to a role, but I don't wander around thinking, "You know, I really should be playing a gruff but fair, deeply-conflicted sheriff in a 19th century mining town…." But when I was living in Boston, I used to audition for TV commercials, and in fact landed a few. (That's right, I was the Fox-25 McDonald's "Burger of the Month" spokesman. Please hold your applause.)

I'd always end up at the same auditions with the same group of my comedian friends, all of us up for the same roles, seeing each other in the same waiting rooms. And there was never much stress about it, at least, not from me, because it wasn't necessarily something I wanted to pursue. I was just looking for exposure for my stand-up, and of course, some extra cash.

At one such casting call, I was sitting with a bunch of my friends, waiting to go in and read for a small commercial part. When I was called in, what nobody realized was that the door separating the waiting room from the audition hall was accidentally left ajar, and thus everyone in the waiting room could overhear everything. There were four or five people in the hall, the Director, Writer, Producer, etc., all sitting behind a table. Very standard stuff. And they were friendly, and said thanks for coming in, we love your comedy, and so forth.

Then the director said, "We're looking for a high energy, manic sort of reading for this character, can you give us that?"

And I said, "Oh, I'm definitely not the guy you're looking for. "

There was a moment of stunned silence, then one of them said, "Wow. We've never heard that from someone auditioning before." And I replied, "Well, I just wanted to be honest, I'm not a high-energy, jumping around kind of guy, and I don't want to waste your time." Another pause, then: "Well, we really appreciate your candor, Ed. So, could we ask you to do the reading in a way that's more your style?"

So that's what I did, and when I went back through the waiting room as I was leaving, all my friends had heard the entire exchange and couldn't stop laughing at what I'd said. To this day, I have Boston friends who still will randomly say to me, *"Oh, I'm definitely not the guy you're looking for!"*

Anyway, back in David's office, I launched into my latest version of the "Oh, I'm not your guy" speech, but Hoberman cut me off. "No, I really would like you to read for this. Will you?" he asked. "But, I'm not a classical actor type, I mean, I know how to act, but I basically have to be playing myself. Your lead is a detective!", I sputtered. Though amused by my hesitance, David was undeterred. "I'd really like to see you read for the role, just being yourself. What do you say?" Well what *could* I say? "Of course I will," I replied.

After the meeting, I called my manager, Ahmos, and shouted, "He wants me to act in the show!"

"Well, that's great!"

"No, it isn't! Come on, I'm not a 'leading man' type, it's not even a comedy, it's a drama."

"This will be good for you," he shot back. And I knew he was right, but it all struck me as a bit absurd. "Obviously, I have to do it," I admitted.

I thought back to the very first acting I ever did, when I wrote myself into some sketches for the comedy troupe *Cross Comedy*, and how the experience of acting actually helped make me a better writer and comedian. So, this would be a good experience if I'll allow it to be, right?

"We should hire you an acting coach!" Ahmos opined.

"Well, you seem to be suggesting I'm not an actor. You know, like I've been saying!"

"No, it will help."

"Look, Hoberman said he wants me to be me, and I have experience in that area. Just let me do this my way, okay?"

I determined that I would just take this as a fun opportunity, try not to stress out, and just have fun with it. In reality, there was nothing riding on it.

There was no way I was going to be chosen as the lead on a network drama, so I might as well just enjoy the process.

Hoberman's people sent me the sides, which is to say, not the entire pilot, but just some scenes. Typically, these may actually be in the pilot, but often are simply scenes written for audition purposes. As I read them, I mused, *these are really good. Wow, these guys really don't need my help with the writing. Exceptional stuff.* And while I didn't hire an acting coach, I did however rehearse the scenes with some real actors I know, which was extremely helpful. I just played the character as me, as David had requested.

A week later, I was back in David's office, performing the three scenes. It was just me and him, and he played the roles of all the other characters in the script. But it was my character, the lead, who understandably had the majority of the lines. It was nerve-wracking in some ways, but relaxed in other ways because again, I knew I had no chance of getting the role, so why be nervous? And my performance was funny enough so that if there ever did come a time when they decided they wanted a wise-cracking bartender or something on the show, they'd think of me.

After I finished, David looked at me with a smile.

Uh oh, I thought. Did he think that sucked, and he's gonna say, 'Wow, you weren't lying when you said you couldn't do this?'

I held my breath, then he said, "That was really good, Ed."

"Yeah? Geez, thanks. Just being myself."

He nodded. "Really good, Ed. I'm not just saying that to make you feel good. Seriously, you're one of the best people we've seen for the role so far."

And *that* is the moment when I really started panicking.

Holy crap. He's serious. Oh my God. This is terrifying. That's what I thought, but I obviously didn't say it. "I don't know what to say, that's really nice to hear," I sputtered.

I left the audition and called my manager, and I guess I sounded disconsolate.

"What, did you bomb or something?" he asked.

"Apparently not," I replied, and explained what had occurred.

For once in my career, I was actually worried about *not* being rejected for a project. I really didn't feel it was something that I was qualified for overall, and it had me pretty wound up. (Does this make any sense to you, reader? I hope so. It probably reads kind of absurd, but what can I say? It's what I was feeling.) If it was, "Can you be the lead in a show about a comedian?" I'd say, "Sure!" But this felt outside my aegis, and certainly outside my comfort zone (as small as that mythical area actually is.)

About a month later, David called to tell me that alas, he'd hired some dude named Tony Shaloub. Honestly, I wasn't disappointed, I was relieved! Especially to lose out to a real actor who is tremendous. I'll admit, if it had been some other comedian who wasn't really an actor, just like me, I'd probably have been ticked off. And obviously if I'd actually landed the role, it would have been a huge career boost, no matter how well the show ultimately did or didn't do in the ratings. But this truly felt like the best outcome.

As fate would have it, *Monk* ran on USA Network for eight years, garnering a slew of awards including Emmys and Golden Globes. Yet I'm still relieved, honestly!

* * * *

One of the most thrilling meetings I've ever had was with the great Bob Newhart. My manager had run into Bob's manager one evening in Las Vegas, and found out that Bob was doing a roast of his friend Don Rickles, and was looking for someone to help him write some jokes for the event. Obviously, Bob's a comedic genius, but even comedic geniuses like to have some help for certain occasions. Being a good manager, Ahmos urged Bob's rep to have his client look at some of my writing samples. (I didn't know any of this was happening, because Ahmos didn't want to get my hopes up if things didn't work out.)

Fortunately, Ahmos called and told me that Newhart had read my stuff and really liked it, and wanted to work with me. Was it okay if Bob called me at home? Uh, yeah, I'm cool with that!

My phone rang and I heard that familiar voice. You know, the one from TV! I don't normally get star struck, but it's *Bob Freakin' Newhart!* He's truly a comedy icon. It was so amazing to be chatting with him, and he asked if I'd write some material, print it out, and bring it to his house where we could go over it. Is that okay? It sure is.

A few days later, I made my way to Bob's house, tucked away in yet another LA canyon. Even with GPS, the roads in these areas can be very confusing, and as per usual, I was struggling to find the exact address. Much like the first time I went to Billy Crystal's house, I was getting increasingly nervous that I would be late. (Hey, at least I didn't have to pee. Yet.)

Luckily, unlike that adventure, it was daytime, and not raining, and I finally realized I had just driven past the correct house. In my haste to turn around in front of his place, I ended up smashing into his trash cans at the curb, scattering them loudly about the pavement. At least they were empty, but the noise they made was incredible. It sounded as though someone had set up a drum circle in the street. I could actually see neighbors peering out of their windows to see what the racket was all about. Another great entrance made by yours truly.

I rang the bell, and Bob himself answered. I immediately blurted out, "I have to tell you, I was a bit nervous pulling up and I… ended up knocking your trash cans all over the place."

He looked at me stoically, then asked, "Did you pick them up?"

"Of course," I answered.

"Great, come on in," he answered in that classic, deadpan delivery.

He turned out to be a lovely guy, just as friendly and down to earth as one could hope. When I handed him the material I'd written, he started perusing it, then suddenly looked at me.

"Uh, Ed, you won't, uh, be insulted if I'm not laughing out loud while I'm reading these, will you?" he asked.

"I'll be *surprised*, but not insulted!" I answered, and he chuckled.

It was extremely considerate of him to even ask, but as a comic myself, I knew how we rarely actually laugh out loud when working on material as a group, no matter how funny it might be. Most folks would be surprised at how clinical comedy writing can be, where we'll excitedly say, "Oh, that's funny!" and focus on how to keep improving it, as opposed to actually laughing.

Anyway, he read through my stuff, giving me several oh-that's-funnys, which made me feel great. At my prompting, he also regaled me with fabulous stories of his adventures with Don Rickles over the years. Amazingly, Bob and his wife Ginny went on vacation with Don and his wife Barbara every year. My favorite thing Bob said to me, in his understated way, was "As you can imagine, Ed, Don has a hard time relaxing." Yes, I can definitely imagine that.

It was so much fun chatting about comedy, and life, and I could've stayed there all day. But eventually, Bob said, "So, okay, do we feel like we're set with what we need?", which I realized was his polite way of saying, "Beat it, kid," so I made my way out. He walked me to the door, then after we said our good-byes, he suddenly called after me: "Hey Ed, you uh, might want to be careful. Apparently, we have some feral trash cans roaming the neighborhood, and from what I've heard, they can leap in front of your car with no warning!"

* * * *

And now, a few other magical moments from various "showbiz" business meetings:

- I met with the head of a production company regarding a new show they were developing. When I was escorted into his office, I noticed luggage and dry cleaning hanging up everywhere. "What, are you fleeing the country?" I joked.

  "I am leaving the country, heading to Hawaii," he replied.

  "But Hawaii is still part of our country, right? Or did I miss some big news this morning?" I teased. He looked at me blankly, then launched into a pitch about his new show. He was giving off really odd vibes. He seemed as nervous as he was humorless. I drove home from the meeting thinking, "Well, that was weird." The next day, it was all over the news that this guy and his wife were arrested for embezzling from their own production company. (I wonder if Hawaii has an extradition treaty with the United States?)

- After yet another strange encounter with a booze-breathed Executive Producer regarding his show, I couldn't wait to leave. I was backing out of the parking lot when the friendly attendant called out, "How'd it go?" At that exact moment, I maneuvered too close to a pole and ripped my driver's side mirror completely off. "Pretty much like that," I told him.

- I agreed to be an EP - Head Writer on a series that a production company was pitching to various studios. It involved baseball player Jose Canseco as the host, and would feature him challenging professional athletes from all sports to various athletic activities (running, swimming, boxing, etc.) Canseco was best known as being one of the first players to admit to steroid use, and to declare its prevalence throughout the league. (I know, it's like the universe decided for some inexplicable reason that I should do as many TV programs with folks who use PEDs as possible.) History had ultimately proven Canseco correct regarding how widespread steroid use truly was, and it seemed like every studio in Hollywood wanted to meet with us. Consequently, we figured we had a good chance of getting the show on the air. But after meeting with at least fifteen networks and studios, we began to realize: nobody really wanted to actually greenlight the show. They just wanted to meet Canseco and hear his thoughts on steroids in baseball. The show never got off the ground. (Maybe we should have injected it with steroids?)

- I was with my agent awaiting a meeting with a studio executive to whom we were going to pitch an idea for a new show. As we huddled nervously in a conference room, awaiting his entrance, my agent suddenly turned to me and whispered, "The thing you have to know about this guy is —" And right then, the "guy" he was talking about bolted into the room, introduced himself, and told us to go ahead with our presentation. Of course, not hearing the rest of what I "have to know about this guy" had me completely disconcerted. I shot a quick look at my agent, in desperate hopes that he could somehow finish conveying his crucial information in some non-verbal way. But he just grinned and nodded, as if to say, "Go ahead, Ed, dazzle him!"

My mind immediately flashed to a writing team I know. As they were going into a meeting with an executive, one writer said to his partner, "This guy is deaf in his left ear, so make sure you speak more towards his right side." So the other writer spent the entire pitch contorting himself to make sure he was speaking into the executive's right ear, drawing some odd looks from the exec. Things seemed to go fine, and in the elevator on the way out, the first writer turned to the second and said, "Good job. Though he was getting weirded out the way you kept moving to his one side." The second writer replied, "But you said he was deaf in his left ear!" And the first writer said, "Oh, I made that up. His hearing is fine, you looked like an idiot!" and laughed in his partner's face. (The only thing worse than a comedy writer is *two* comedy writers.)

Anyway, I finished the pitch, it seemed to go well, then as we were exiting the building, I asked my agent, "What where you going to say that I needed to know about him?" He looked at me blankly, then said, "Oh, I don't remember." Well, thanks for the extra adrenaline jolt for the presentation, anyway.

- I got to do a quick project with the late, great Joan Rivers. The first voicemail I ever got from her said, "Ed, this is Joan Rivers. So far, I'm not laughing. But we haven't even met yet, so I'll give you a break on that. Will you come see me at my place?" She left her address, and I drove over to her house. When she answered the door, I said, "Hey, gotta say, it's an honor." And she said, "Yeah, right! Don't schmooze me!" Hilarious. And when I handed her some material I'd written for her, she said, "Hey, these are really funny!" And I snapped, "Damn right they are! Don't sound so surprised, who do you think I am? It's what I do!" She howled, and I realized that irreverence was a shared mutual trait. A fun project, and she of course is missed.

- Speaking of legends, a few years back, Martin Short was putting together a variety show, and amazingly, he was interested in having me as one of his Head Writers. I was lucky enough that I was actually being pursued by another show at the same time, which happened to have a bigger budget, but man, Martin Short? I wanted to at least meet him. So we had an amazing dinner in Beverly Hills. Not surprisingly, he was witty, charming, and incredibly creative on the fly. He's truly an amazing talent. He knew I was being courted by another show, and said he understood that I'd ultimately have to choose whichever was best for me and my family. A very gracious guy. As we parted, he gave me his home number and asked that I call him, no matter what I decided. As it turned out, the other offer I'd received was just too good to pass up, and it was with great reluctance that I found myself having to call him to decline the gig.

He was classy of course, which somehow made me feel even worse about my decision. Alas, for reasons that weren't his fault, his show unfortunately didn't last long, and also unfortunately, neither did the show I'd turned his down for. All I could think was, yet another perfect microcosm of the entertainment industry.

What about meetings with folks that were unplanned, and worse yet, I didn't even recognize them? It's happened more than once. For instance:

- I was performing at a club with comedian Jonathan Katz, and backstage after my set, I ran into one of Jonathan's friends who'd tagged along for the evening. He introduced himself as Dave, and was full of effusive praise for my show, which I thanked him for. We chatted for a bit, then I went back out into the showroom to watch some of Jonathan's set. The club manager approached me and said, "Hey, David Mamet is in the audience. And he told me he loved your show." I said, "Seriously? Holy crap, one of the all-time great playwrights liked my show? Wow. Can you bring me to meet him?" The manager said, "For sure, come on, follow me," then proceeded to escort me right over to...Jonathan's friend Dave, whom I had met backstage earlier.

  "Hey, David," the manager said, "Ed wanted to meet you."

  "We've actually met!" Mamet said pleasantly.

  "Uh, wow, seriously, I feel stupid," I replied. "You're praising me for things like jokes about grocery stores, and I don't even realize I'm talking to a Pulitzer-prize winner. I'm sorry I didn't recognize you!"

  Mamet laughed and said, "Aw, why would you? And at least you were nice to me, right?"

  It turns out Mamet and Katz were roommates back in college. I told Jonathan the story after his show, and how mortified I was that I didn't know who I was talking to. At the very least, I could have returned the compliments! Katz cracked up and assured me that Mamet really doesn't particularly like being recognized, so all was good. Like so many moments in show biz, it was both awesome yet cringey at the same time. (Come to think of it, not an unfamiliar theme in my life in general.)

- Once when I was having dinner with David Steinberg, a man approached our table and greeted David warmly. I said hello as well, but there were no introductions because he and David immediately got into a big conversation. As I was studying this guy, I kept thinking, okay, what show do I know him from? Maybe a bunch of different shows? Movies? TV? Both? I noticed other diners sneaking occasional glances at him as well, which confirmed my suspicion that he was definitely a public figure. I finally decided he was on one of those very popular soap operas, but I wasn't sure which one. After he and David finished their discussion, we all started making small talk, and I finally said, "Hey, I apologize, which show are you on? I can't think of it." There was a small pause, then he and David burst out laughing. And so, I started laughing as well, even though I didn't really understand why that was funny. That is, until a couple men in suits came over and said, "Mayor Reardon, we need to get you to your press conference." The "soap actor" turned out to be Richard Reardon, mayor of LA. Luckily, when you're a comedian, people think you're joking even when you aren't. I didn't have the nerve to tell Steinberg that I'd been serious when asking about which soap his friend was on.

- One very late night, I was wandering the grounds of CBS Radford Studios, feeling sorry for myself over what just seemed so damn important at the moment. I was hosting a show for HBO Workspace and at the last minute, one of my scheduled guests had unexpectedly dropped out the day before the taping. I was strolling along with

Jason, one of my Producers, just venting about who we were going to get on such short notice. As Jason patiently listened to my frustrated discourse, we suddenly passed another guy strolling by us. He called out, "How's it going, guys?" so I interrupted my complaining for a moment to politely nod greetings back to him. The guy walked over to his car, got in, and drove away, and I immediately went back to my lamenting about our guest predicament. Jason said, "Well, why didn't you ask him?", referring to the stranger we'd just barely encountered. I was a little irritated by Jason's glibness, and barked, "Oh, is that where we're at now? Just asking random strangers to be on the show? That's great!" Jason stopped walking. "Did you see who that was?" he asked.

"No. Did you know the guy?"

"I don't know him," Jason replied. "But I know who he is. John Travolta."

Yikes. If he'd still been there, I'd definitely have asked him! No doubt he'd probably have turned me down, but one never knows, right? I admire God's sense of humor. I'm asking for a last-minute fill-in, He walks Travolta *almost right into me*, but I'm too busy complaining that I can't find a guest star to even recognize him.

CHAPTER 4
Musical Notes are Better than Network Notes

I 've always loved music. From the time I first learned to play guitar (fifth grade), until the time I realized I could never be a professional musician (fifth grade), I have always found music to be one of the greatest joys on earth, along with elastic waist jeans. Thus, I am always excited when I have an opportunity to work with a musician. Whether it's doing standup as their opening act, or writing jokes for their in-between-songs patter, or helping shape the structure of their television special, I love it all.

There's no doubt that music and laughter go together like, well, laughter and music. I'm guessing most teenagers did—and still do—enjoy making up silly lyrics to popular songs. Some are wittier than others for sure, though singing "Wang in the Water" instead of "Wade in the Water" in Catholic grade school was a guaranteed laugh, every time. Also popular was the Rush song, "Closer To The Heart," 14-year-old dufus version:

> *"And the men who hold their gas in,*
> *Must be the ones who start,*
> *To pass it with impunity,*
> *And cut a hellish fart…"*

Gold, I tell ya. Gold! And that true staple of my youth, *Mad* magazine, always had lots of fun song parodies, some of which I can still remember word for word, 40 years later, even though I can barely remember my kids' names (and I only have one kid.) A serial killer singing *"Try to dismember, a guy in September,"* or a surgeon singing *"Cruising down the river on a Sunday afternoon,"* as he operates on a patient, still makes me guffaw.

Song parodies in general are looked down upon by many if not most comedy writers, but I always enjoyed some of the funnier ones. Oh, I can be a snob about it as well. Somebody singing *"Ceilings"* to the tune of *"Feelings"* isn't that clever to me, but if there's more to the parody than just that, I'm open to it. I used to perform song parodies when I first started doing standup, but didn't feel like shlepping my guitar to every club I played, so I eventually jettisoned them from my act. But I've continued to write parodies for other acts over the years, and I always find it fun.

The best of those times was helping Billy Crystal with his song parodies of the films nominated for Best Picture at the Oscars. It was always put together by musician-composer Marc Shaiman, winner of many illustrious awards including a Tony, Grammy, and an Emmy. The writers would gather at Marc's house in the hills above Hollywood and riff away, laughing and singing as Marc played the piano. Lots of fun. Not to mention, we put together some great comedic medleys for the *Academy Awards.* As you might imagine, some of the funniest ones we had to keep to ourselves, but we always managed to have some great ones suitable for the actual telecast.

You never knew who might interrupt a session with Marc with an urgent phone call, which he'd usually just answer on speaker while we continued to work. Once when I was there, the phone rang and we heard, "Hi Marc, it's Bette Midler." Forgetting that we were on speaker, I blurted out, "Who? Never heard of you!" It was totally silent, and everyone looked at me. Then from the phone we heard, "Who is that?" Well, in for a penny, in for a pound.

"It's Ed Driscoll" I piped up.

"Who?" came the voice from the phone again.

"That's Ed, one of Billy's writers," Marc interjected, laughing.

"Do I know you?" came the voice from the phone. Now everyone was snickering.

"Uh, no, fortunately, you don't!" I answered back, then mercifully Marc took the call in the other room.

Another cool thing about doing those songs with Billy was the fact we'd rehearse them with a full orchestra, sometimes over at the famous Capitol Records building in Hollywood. You can just feel the history emanating from its walls. Artists such as Frank Sinatra, Nat King Cole, Michael Jackson, Dean Martin, Barbra Streisand, Paul McCartney, and The Beach Boys have all recorded there. (Interestingly, my dentist's office is located right across the street, so if I ever thought a long rehearsal felt like pulling teeth, I could always dash across the street for a reminder of what that feeling is *really* like.)

*   *   *   *

I also wrote lyrics for songs on other shows, including the theme song to the animated show *Ozzy & Drix*, along with brilliant composer Randall Crissman. I eventually became a member of the American Society of Composers, Authors, and Publishers. (As a side note, ASCAP was the only one of my three unions — though technically, ASCAP is a membership organization — that didn't go on strike in 2023. More on labor situations later.)

I was also known in writers rooms for bursting into song at odd times with lyrics inspired by whatever insane moment was happening in our world. Again, many of those will have to stay between me and my fellow scribes, for everyone's protection. (But I'll sing you some in person sometime, if you'd like.)

Due to my "musical reputation" — but mostly thanks to a recommendation from my hilarious friend, comedian Larry Amoros, Barry Manilow's chief writer — I was hired to help put together Barry's first residence show at the Las Vegas Hilton. Barry's one of those songwriters that you kind of forget that he has that many hits. You think, yeah, I like a couple of his songs.

Then you think, oh, and that one, too. Oh yeah, I forgot about that one, too. Oh, and that one. Then as one after another pops into your head, you realize, damn, this guy's prolific. In fact, the song for the first dance for my bride and myself at our wedding was "Weekend in New England." (As I did with Tom Bergeron, I eventually stopped blaming Barry for my marriage as well. But as with Tom, it took me some time.)

Seriously though, he turned out to be not only prolific but extremely nice, too. A total pleasure to work with. He has a great sense of humor, and he really knows how to deliver a line in his own natural, New York rhythm. And my favorite part about him was the way he'd turn down a joke that he didn't want to use. I'd pitch him a line, and he'd say, "That's really funny, Ed, but I don't think that would work for me." If only *all* the people I worked with were as polite when turning down a joke. Maybe then I'd need to see my shrink only *once* a week.

We did a week of "previews," which are basically public performances that take place before the official opening of a show. It's a chance to identify possible problem areas and make improvements based on audience reactions. As I stood backstage watching the crowd file into the theater, it was always amusing to see guys who appeared to be dragged reluctantly to see Barry Manilow by their wives and girlfriends. You could see they were resentful by their general demeanor as they took their seats prior to the show. And yet, by the third song, those same guys would be up in the aisles dancing and singing along. Now it was the ladies' turn to feel embarrassed!

Once the official opening week arrived, there were posters everywhere throughout the hotel, and Barry's music was constantly playing in the elevators and lobbies of the casino. Barry made an offhand quip that "Well, I guess it's official, my songs are elevator music." We laughed, and I said, "You should just tell the crowd, hey, if you want to hear my show and save the sixty bucks, just ride the elevators for an hour." He ended up using the line on stage, which was fun.

Another fun part was the old-school celebs that would drop by Barry's dressing room from time to time. Suzanne Sommers, Diane Sawyer, Elton John. Sir Elton actually was accompanied by a guy who cares for his toupee, Wiggy. Seriously. (I assumed it was a nickname, but who knows, it could be an informal version of "Wiggledon" or something.) I have to say, it is the best hairpiece I've ever seen. There's no way you'd know it was fake, other than Sir Elton talking about it publicly himself from time to time, with a good sense of humor about it. Man, what a way to make a living. *And what do you do?* "*Oh, I handle Elton John's hair.*" Great work, if you can get it.

*   *   *   *

In 2010, I got my first opportunity to work with one of my very favorite singers, Michael Bublé. I've been a fan since I first heard him, so I jumped at the chance to accompany him on tour for a bit and help write patter and song introductions and the like. I checked into the hotel in Florida where we were staying for the first nights of rehearsal, and met Michael in the restaurant for a casual conversation.

He couldn't have been nicer. (Okay, I guess that's an inaccurate way to describe anyone. I suppose someone can *always* somehow be nicer. I mean, him handing me a million dollars would have been even nicer. But barring that unlikely event, he was pretty damn close to being unable to be nicer.) We had a great chat, and I found him very down to earth. And although he didn't actually hand me a million dollars, he did actually say, "I love your ideas, Ed. I sure hope you're getting paid a lot!" (I made a mental note to fire my agent and hire Michael in his place.)

The following morning, I was sitting in the lobby of the hotel awaiting my ride to the show venue when the elevator doors opened and out stepped Michael. No entourage, nobody else, just him. He spotted me and called out, "Ed, I'm walking over to get some Starbucks, can I bring you anything?" I was taken aback. For one thing, I was surprised that he'd be fetching his own coffee. Most people in his position would send out an assistant for that task.

And secondly, I couldn't believe that he was offering to bring *me* some coffee, as if he was *my* assistant or something. Such a completely nice, grounded guy. How the hell could he be in the entertainment industry?

I replied, "Uh, no, but thank you. I'm about to head over to the stage." "Okay, see you over there!" he answered cheerfully, and exited the hotel. I sat there thinking wow, honestly, I'm not sure I would've gotten coffee for *him*. He's clearly nicer than me!

We met up later backstage at the venue, and chatted about some possible lines to test out during rehearsal. Then I took my seat in the theatre, and sat back and listened to Michael and the band do their thing. Wow, they were not holding back, they were letting it rip. I was in awe. Besides the great musicians on stage, I was stunned to hear how incredible Bublé's voice actually is. I mean, we all know it's good, but it's pretty rare for a singer to be even better live than they are in their studio recordings. It's honestly the best, natural singing voice I've ever heard in my life, and I have heard some great ones.

His manager came over and sat next to me. I looked at him, and he knew what I was thinking. "Pretty good voice, huh?" he chuckled. "Wow," I said. "It's unreal." He smiled and said, "Yeah, I used to be worried that he'd blow his voice out in some of these rehearsals before he even had a chance to do the show, but he always belts it out and never seems to falter."

We watched a couple more songs, then I said, "So tell me, seriously, is he really as nice as he appears to be?" He chuckled again, and said, almost in bewilderment, "Yes, that's him. He just loves people." "Well, he must not be around enough of them," I joked. "But seriously, that's great."

Michael likes to tell a story onstage about his grandfather. Back in Canada, when Michael was only sixteen, his grandpa, who was a plumber, would sometimes exchange free plumbing work for local nightclub owners if they'd allow his underage grandson to sing onstage from time to time. It was evident at a very young age that Bublé had a rare talent, and the love and support from his grandpa helped nurture him to become the singer, and the person, he'd become. His grandpa was still alive, and whenever possible, he'd come to Michael's concerts, no matter where they were being held. In fact, Michael told me he was excited that his grandpa was arriving later that afternoon to spend a few days and catch the shows. They hadn't seen each other in a bit, and they were looking forward to catching up.

In the early evening, after the last rehearsal, I went to the dining area set up backstage for musicians and the rest of the crew. After loading up my plate, I turned and noticed that Michael and his grandfather were sitting at a table chatting excitedly. I smiled and thought, aw, cool, glad they're together. And not wanting to interrupt anything, I sat a few tables away by myself, to give them some privacy.

After a few minutes, Michael spotted me and called out, "Ed! Why are you sitting over there by yourself?" "Oh, I don't mind at all," I replied. "I wanted to give you a chance to visit with your family." He smiled and said, "Well, you're family now, too. Get over here!" I truly didn't want to intrude, but apparently he didn't see my presence as an intrusion, so I shyly made my way to their table and finished my dinner with them. As we ate dessert, I said, "Listen, now that I'm officially part of the family, can I borrow some money?" They laughed, and I didn't have the heart to tell them I wasn't kidding.

CHAPTER 5

Laboring for Laughs

As a member of both the Writers Guild of America and the Screen Actors Guild, I've been involved in two major labor disputes since 1994. Writers struck for 100 days in 2007-08 to secure pay for content distributed online, even while the studios claimed that they didn't think this whole internets-thingie would last. They begrudgingly agreed to a few extra pennies for our work that would appear on this "new medium." And it's a good thing we got our foot in the door regarding web content back then, because by 2023, the studios were making billions via streaming and posting content on that whole internets-thingie. Yet they still pretended as though they were uncertain about whether people would actually watch content online.

I've observed warily over the years as more and more of the entertainment industry has been taken over by corporations. Make no mistake, when Hollywood was run by people like Jack Warner, Louie B. Mayer, and Sam Goldwyn, those guys were SOBs to negotiate with. However, they were part of the entertainment *community*. Their kids went to school with the children of writers, actors, and crew members, and they all knew each other socially. No matter how tough-minded these executives were, at the end of the day, they had a vested interest in the entertainment industry itself, and actually cared about putting out a quality product.

But these days, studios are merely divisions of mega corporations, just like refrigerators or auto parts. Instead of decision-makers who are part of the process, we have bean counters sent from Manhattan to LA to cut creative staff in order to appease their Wall Street overlords. Then, after wreaking havoc on the creative process, they make their triumphant return to their East Coast offices to announce, "I forced them to cut their writing staff in half, but still produce the same amount of work, for the same salary! Where's my bonus?" I wish this was an exaggeration.

In 2007, with my usual impeccable timing, I was the host of *Behind The Lines with Ed Driscoll*, a pilot directed by the wonderful Troy Miller. It was a show featuring a panel of comedy writers, swapping stories of our adventures in "the room." It turned out great, and we had high hopes for selling it to a network. And that's exactly when the writers went on strike. And once things were settled in 2008, pretty much the last thing any studio exec wanted was a show about these damn writers, who they blamed for the strike, and for being extremely greedy people. (And you thought "projection" in Hollywood was only done in movie theaters.)

In 2008, social media was still in its infancy, and the studios were able to control the public narrative since they controlled the mainstream press. They did their best to portray the writers as ungrateful punks not satisfied with making actual money for merely creating, writing, and producing the "content" that was in fact making the studios wealthy beyond belief. And sadly, a large percentage of the general public was fooled by what they heard and read, and support for the embarrassingly exploited workers was at best fifty percent by anyone outside of the industry.

But by 2023, writers were able to get past the desperate gatekeepers beholden to the studio executives and simply present the facts of why there was another strike by writers and actors. And as the public was given the actual facts of the situation — not hyperbole, but straight numbers — public sentiment sided overwhelmingly with the workers.

Writers' pay over the last five years has declined by 14%, yet studio and network CEO pay has increased by 50%. In 2022, Warner Bros. Discovery boss David Zaslav made $246.6 million. Bob Iger of Disney made $45.9

million. Paramount CEO Bob Bakish made $32 million. As many have pointed out, even a small portion of each major CEO's annual salary would cover the costs of the writers and performers' asks, yet they say it's not possible. But obviously, it's very possible. The fact is, the AMPTP — the negotiators working on behalf of studio and corporate interests — would prefer to break the unions than offer them another crumb. Think that's just my biased opinion? Well, check out these statements as reported by *Deadline Hollywood*:

"The endgame is to allow things to drag on until union members start losing their apartments and losing their houses," a studio executive told Deadline. Acknowledging the cold-as-ice approach, several other sources reiterated the statement. One insider called it "a cruel but necessary evil."

Seriously. If a screenwriter had written those lines for some superhero movie villain, they'd have been scolded by Producers for dialogue so "over-the-top." Nobody would ever actually say that, right? And yet, they did. And not just in private. Right in front of reporters. They *wanted* that message to get out there, to intimidate labor. Of course, the mouth-breathers who actually said these things didn't have the courage to be named on the record. And as *Lost* writer Javier Grillo-Marxuach pointed out, "They (the studios and networks) shut down an entire industry rather than part with less than 3% of their record profits."

Now, I understand what some people think when they see some of the salaries writers can command (though few seem to realize that it's a very small percentage of writers who are making enormous sums of money.) I'll put it this way. I'll admit that years ago, when I first heard of professional athletes going on strike, I thought, wow, what greedy jerks. They're being paid millions to play a game! But once I understood that the owners were making *billions* from the work done by these same players, I realized, there's no reason for the players not to make a fair bulk of that money. Now of course, teachers, firefighters, etc. are far more important for society, and it would be great for them to all make more money. But the sobering fact is, rock stars, athletes, actors, and other entertainers make a lot more money for their employers than other, far more necessary jobs bring in. It's just how it is. But personally, I'd rather have more of my baseball ticket money go to the guys actually playing the game than to some entitled, billionaire owner who mostly views his team as a tax write-off.

The CEOs of the studios and their cronies tell stockholders that the future of streaming is bright, and worth investing in. Yet they tell the writers that streaming is an uncertain future, and thus they can't make reasonable deals at this time. Well, which is it, folks?

The truth is, all of us in the industry had seen this coming. Despite reaching an agreement in 2008, during the last decade or so we've watched with concern as the studios continued to pull all kinds of sleazy tricks. Such as, taking two brand new writers fresh out of college, pairing them up even though they don't know each other, and calling them a "writing team," in order to pay them one writer's salary, that they're then forced to split. *"You don't like it? Too bad, that's our offer, take it or leave it. There's a lot of people who'd kill for this chance!"* (Well, if that's the case, maybe one of those people will kill the heartless bastard who came up with the entire "writing team" scam in the first place?)

Also, the reason some of your favorite shows are often cancelled after a few seasons is not because the show is unsuccessful. Sometimes, it's actually because the shows *are* successful, which under ordinary contracts, means the cast and crew — in other words, the people who do the actual work — are given automatic pay bumps with each new season. As incredible as it may sound, networks often cancel these shows prematurely just to avoid paying the salary bumps they'd promised in the contracts.

Not to say that studio greed and avarice are the issues here, but…they are. The reluctance, and outright refusal, of studios to reasonably share their millions of dollars in profits with the very people who have made those profits possible is unconscionable.

Fortunately, the 2023 strike did eventually end, with the unions getting a reasonable deal when all was said and done. But the sad part is, it was a deal that could have been agreed to without a strike at all, had the AMPTP been interested in keeping the industry alive, rather than attempting to crush labor in order to get an even bigger slice of the pie that's created by said labor.

Oh, remember the story I said I'd "circle back" to you with, about getting stiffed on my pay for a Netflix show? Well, it doesn't matter if you don't, the production company claims not to remember, either. But I do, so let me tell you about it. (And it's a classic example of the type of things happening in our industry that led to the inevitable labor dispute in 2023.)

The contract I had with that particular show involved me producing and writing all of the show's episodes over the course of eight weeks. As I tend to do, I worked quickly and efficiently, so much so that with one week left in the production, I'd basically finished all the work I'd been hired to do.

It was Friday of week seven when the Executive Producer came sauntering into my office.

"Hey, I wanted to talk to you for a minute," he began.

"Of course, what's up?"

"Well, I was just thinking, you really don't need to come in next week. We're nicely set to finish the series."

There was something about the way he said it that made me feel a bit uneasy.

"What, am I fired?" I asked jokingly.

"No, of course not. You've been amazing. I hope you'll come back and work a second season if we get one. It's just that we really don't need you next week in the studio."

There was an awkward pause, then I said, "Well, my contract is for eight weeks, so I'm happy to come in for the last week and supervise and do whatever I can to help out where it's needed."

But he assured me that wasn't necessary, and even mentioned that I'd probably be relieved not having to make the hellish, traffic-clogged drive anymore. He was right about that, of course. But something seemed off.

"Well, just let me know if you change your mind," I offered, and he thanked me and exited. I picked up the phone and called my agent. I told him about the discussion I'd just had, and said, "Look, I just want us to make sure they're not simply trying to get out of paying me my last week's salary. Because I'll show up every day next week, even if they claim they don't need me to. Because I'm not getting stiffed on our agreement."

My agent understood my concern, and said he'd check in with the show's contract people. He called me back minutes later, and said he'd been reassured by the show's representatives that of course I'd be getting my last week's salary, and I really didn't need to come in at all next week. Hey, fine by me. Especially when a lot of the folks I'd been working with there were not exactly the friendliest group I'd been around.

The next week, I stayed home, but I called into the studio several times, just to check in, and see if I could help with a line or idea or whatever they might need. I made a couple minor pitches they requested, and that was that. I mean, even though they didn't require me to be there in person, we were still under contract, and I wanted to be professional.

As incredible as it all might seem…well, you probably see where this is going. After not receiving my final payment for several weeks, my agent informed me that they'd gotten into an argument with the show's accountants, and yes indeed, the show was trying to screw me out of my last week's paycheck.

Mind you, this was a multi-million-dollar production, and they only owed me—what was for them—peanuts. A mere four figures. I was basically being punished for doing all my work in less time than they thought I'd require.

I mentioned to my agent that I happened to see a receipt for wine and champagne that was purchased for the studio executives, for a party celebrating the wrapping of the show. It was 10 thousand dollars. More than what they owed me.

The show's lawyers basically told my agent that sure, we could sue for the money, but it would cost us more in legal fees than it would be worth. Seriously. That was their bargaining stance.

This wasn't really Netflix screwing me over, it was these particular Producers. But Netflix certainly could have made them live up to their agreement, but they were too busy cashing checks to care when we brought it to their attention.

Ultimately, the show begrudgingly sent me a payment that was about one-third of what they owed me, and acted as though I should be grateful that they even did that. Well, as long as the executives got enough champagne, I'm pleased I was able to contribute.

*   *   *   *

Okay, well, sorry reader, didn't mean to bring us all down. Thanks for letting me vent. I don't mean to sound ungrateful regarding the entertainment industry. To quote *The Godfather,* "This is the business we've chosen." And to paraphrase Churchill, "It's the worst business in the world —except for all the rest of them."

How about one of the far less depressing aspects of walking the picket lines? I think my favorite story is from the 2008 strike. I had a two-year-old, and my four-year-old marriage was already fraying. And the entire industry was shut down, and I had no money coming in, and—wait, how is this less depressing? Oh, yeah, well, one afternoon I was walking the picket line at NBC in Burbank. My wife was out of town, so I brought my two-year-old with me and pushed her in a stroller as we walked back and forth on the sidewalk. I got to chatting with an incredibly nice man named Jerry Maren, who was actually one of the original Munchkins from *Wizard of Oz*. How cool is that?! I kidded with him about me representing the Writers Guild, and he the Lollipop Guild. He jokingly asked me if I had another stroller he could ride in. A funny and nice man, a wonderful human.

As we parted ways when our shift had ended, Jerry asked me if he could give my daughter a kiss on top of her head so that when she got older, I could tell her she was kissed by an actual Munchkin. Absolutely! Ten years later, Jerry passed at age 98, the last surviving cast member from the movie. And my kid does indeed think it's beyond cool that she was kissed by a real Munchkin.

CHAPTER 6
Closing Scenes & Final Curtains

Afew years ago, I guest-hosted a popular LA radio show alongside David Steinberg. It was a four hour show of no music, just talk, and taking call-ins. That can be a lot of time to fill. Before we went on air, I told David that I was concerned about getting enough call-ins to make our discussions interesting. David reassured me that both Billy Crystal and Robin Williams would phone in to talk. I felt a lot better, knowing that we'd have at least a couple segments that we knew would be good. David and I began the show, and made some funny comments about the news that day, then asked for callers. Billy called in, and we had a great interview with him. But as I'd feared, the quality of many of the other phone conversations with members of the general public did not go as smoothly, and often flew off the rails. David and I did our best to be funny about all of it, but it was not an easy time. As the show went on, and we'd just handled three particularly eccentric calls in a row, we went to break. Off air, in exasperation, I said to David, "Wow, there sure are some bizarre people out there, huh? It's frightening. And what's also frightening is, we've still got forty-five minutes to go. When is Robin going to call in?" And David said, "Oh, those last three callers were Robin!" Robin had called in as three separate strange but totally believable characters, and I had no idea.

* * * *

We all miss Robin. And in fact, it's been a rough few years involving deaths among my entertainment industry colleagues and friends, particularly among comedians. Within the last five years we've lost Bob Saget, a wonderful guy, hilarious, kind, who I was lucky enough to work with both as a performer and a writer on his sitcom *Raising Dad.* Norm MacDonald, who I didn't know well, but whenever our paths would cross in Hollywood, he was unfailingly friendly and funny. Gilbert Gottfried, who I worked with only once on a TV show shot in Nashville, where off-stage he was soft-spoken and polite, the very antithesis of his on-stage persona. Richard Lewis, a fellow Ohio State grad who I worked with several times, and kept in touch with until his untimely passing. And even as I'm writing this book, the aforementioned Bob Newhart has now left us. I'm so grateful I got to meet and work with him. Truly a life well-lived sir, and sorry again about the trash cans!

But the two deaths that hit me the hardest: comedian-actor Steve Bean, and the incomparable Louie Anderson.

I first met Steve many years ago when we both were just starting out, at the Funnybone Comedy Club in Pittsburgh. Steve focused more on the acting side of the business as time went on, and he appeared on many, many shows over the years, including *Cheers, Quantum Leap,* and *Ray Donovan.* After bravely fighting off cancer for several years, he passed on January 21, 2019.

We had been roommates in Boston, and lived in the same apartment complex when we both moved to LA. We shared too many silly adventures to count, but I will share one that I told at a benefit we held to raise money for his medical expenses.

As roomies in Boston, we were constantly creating stupid scenarios and playing pranks on each other, because we found it all hilarious. We shared the same twisted, goofball humor, and we made the most of it. One day, Steve came back to the apartment carrying a toaster. I said, "Hey, that's great, we need a toaster." But Steve deadpanned, "Oh no. No. This is *my* toaster. It's not for you. Don't use it, don't look at it, don't even think about it. It's *my* toaster." Of course, this turned into a running gag between us for weeks. He'd wake up in the morning to find me drinking coffee and longingly staring at the toaster, and would warn me off, "Nope, don't do it." Just mindless fun for us both, and it went on for weeks.

Then one day, when I knew Steve wasn't due back to the apartment until later in the afternoon, I had a thought: why don't I unplug the toaster, put it smack dab in the middle of the living room, then, when I hear him coming up the stairs and keying in the door, I'll be hunched over the toaster and whip around shouting a guilty, "I didn't expect you home so soon!"

Again, ridiculous, but we loved stuff like this. So, I put the toaster in the middle of the living room, and I sat there waiting for him to come back in a few hours. (Yep, this was my afternoon. I'm a busy guy.) As I waited, the thought occurred to me: what if, when he comes back and keys in, I'm actually *naked* next to the toaster. As if something *terribly* untoward was taking place. Ooh yeah, that's better. So I stripped down to my underwear and sat patiently awaiting Steve's return.

At last, I heard him trooping up the steps, so I whipped off my underwear, hunched over the toaster, then as he keyed into the apartment and was greeted with this image, I whipped around and in a panicked voice shouted, "I didn't expect you home so soon!" Steve laughed as hard as I've ever seen him laugh. And the only person who laughed harder than Steve was… his girlfriend, who was with him, who I'd not expected.

* * * *

Then, almost incomprehensibly, on the same date, January 21, three years later, my dear friend Louie Anderson passed away. A devastating loss. Not just for me, but for the literally thousands of people that he did kindnesses for that most people don't know about, because Louie wasn't about doing things for good publicity. He was always about helping out anyone and everyone he could, to a fault.

Louie and I did a lot of collaborating professionally, doing standup shows together, as well as various television projects we co-wrote. We had all kinds of adventures, particularly in LA and Las Vegas, where Louie lived the last few years of his life as comedian in residence at various casinos. Again, too many stories to list, at least in this book at this moment, but I will share a couple of favorites.

Louie and I once did standup together at a very cool supper club type of place outside of LA called the Canyon Club. Though the venue sometimes features comedy acts, it's particularly well-known for the amazing list of great musicians that have worked there through the years. Christopher Cross, George Thorogood, Blood, Sweat & Tears, Styx, Pat Benatar, The Foo Fighters, and on and on. Anyway, we had a very fun show. I did thirty minutes or so to open, then Louie wrapped it up with an hour. The crowd was great, and Louie and I were talking about that fact in the backstage lounge when the manager of the club stuck his head in. "Hey guys, Eddie Money is here, and he wants to stop backstage to say hello." Somewhat stupidly, I blurted out, "Eddie Money, the singer?" And the manager looked at me and said, "No, Eddie Money the Amway salesman. Who do you think?" I laughed and said, "Yeah, I get it, it's just I wasn't expecting to be running into Eddie Money, you know?" We laughed and Louie said, "Please, send him back. We'd love to say hello."

Moments later, in came none other than Eddie Money, along with his wife, his daughter, his daughter's boyfriend, and a few other relatives. A really nice group of folks. As time went on, and Eddie's family was chatting amongst themselves, Eddie pulled Louie and I aside, and leaned in conspiratorially. "Hey, can I tell you guys a joke?" he whispered. "You can use it in your act if you want." Louie and I looked at each other, then said, "*Can* you? We *insist!*"

Looking about furtively to make sure nobody in his family was within earshot, he hit us with the following:

"A guy walks into a dive bar and sees a sign on the wall, reading 'Cheese Sandwich, $3.50. Chicken Sandwich, $4.50. Hand-jobs, ten bucks.' He walks over to the woman behind the bar and asks, 'Excuse me, are you the one who gives the hand-jobs?' And she smiles and says, 'I sure am!' And the guy says, 'Okay, can you wash your hands? 'Cuz I'm gonna have the cheese sandwich.' "

It was all so bizarre, and funny. Not just the joke, but the fact that Eddie Money was telling it to us. And all I could think was, wow, Eddie, just what did you see in the acts that Louie and I just did that would make you think, 'Oh, I've got the *perfect* joke for these guys, it will fit in *seamlessly* with the material they're doing!"

For months after that, when Louie would call me, he'd say, "What's up, Eddie, you havin' a cheese sandwich?"

*   *   *   *

There was a terrific act for many years in Las Vegas by the name of Danny Gans. He was a gifted impressionist-singer-dancer, an all-around entertainer. His whole marketing strategy, which was quite smart, was that he didn't travel anywhere outside of Vegas. He didn't do television (outside of an occasional interview with Larry King.) So if you wanted to see his high-energy act, complete with a full orchestra, you could only do it in Vegas. What entertained in Vegas, stayed in Vegas, so to speak. Thus, his shows were always sold out, a very hot ticket in town. Then tragically, at the age of 52, he had a heart attack in the middle of the night and passed away, leaving a wife and three young children. Terribly sad.

Just a few months prior, I'd started writing some comedy material for Danny's act, and I'd travel from LA to Vegas occasionally to watch him perform, and we'd huddle backstage and discuss the material.

One morning I was at my desk at home in LA, writing some more bits for him, when Louie called me.

"Ed, I'm so sorry about Danny!" Louie began.

"What do you mean?" I asked.

"I'm sorry, I thought you'd heard. He passed away last night!"

I was stunned, and sad, and sat there trying to process this. I told Louie I was actually working on some material for Danny right at this very moment. It all felt macabre and creepy. I said, "Well, you'd better watch out, Louie. I wrote material for Robin, and Danny, and I write material for you, too. Apparently I'm killing people now!"

"Oh Eddie, I don't think you're that powerful," he answered softly. "And I think the last thing that's gonna kill me is one of your jokes. I'm figuring the culprit will more likely be something like McDonald's, or Krispy Kreme."

"Fair enough," I answered, appreciating his attempt to lighten the moment.

Louie and I were both invited to a memorial service that was being held in honor of Danny in Vegas, ironically in the Danny Gans Theater they'd just built exclusively for him weeks earlier at the Encore Hotel.

Louie and I made our way into the auditorium and took our seats. It was a bit surreal to be in this theatre where Danny should be doing his shows, and to be surrounded by other guests like Donny & Marie Osmond, Carrottop, Celine Dion, and Blue Man Group (not in costume). As I scanned the room, I suddenly noticed someone who was obviously the classic Hollywood agent-type. A guy in a flashy suit, slicked back hair, stylish glasses, frantically typing away on his phone. I rolled my eyes and whispered to Louie, "Ugh, do you know that guy? Gotta be an agent." Louie looked at the man and shrugged. "No I don't, Eddie." I found myself getting agitated. "I'm telling you, that's an agent. And he probably doesn't even care that Danny died. He's just here to network!"

Louie looked at me and said, "Honestly, Ed, can you just relax? You don't know what the guy's thinking."

"Well, I have a good feel for these things," I shot back self-righteously. "And I'm telling you, if he starts texting during the ceremony, I'm gonna say something."

Naturally, the guy sat down in the empty seat right next to me. I looked over at Louie and he smirked. "I hate show business, you know?" I mumbled to Louie.

"Just focus on the service, okay Ed?" Louie replied with a sigh.

I nodded, but kept watch on the guy out of the corner of my eye.

The service began with the mayor of Las Vegas, Oscar Goodman, thanking everyone for attending. Surprisingly, the agent-dude next to me actually put his phone away. "We're here to honor a great person, performer, husband, and father. He was taken from us way too soon. To begin, I'd like to ask Danny's beloved pastor to come up now and lead us in an opening prayer." And with that, the "agent-guy" that I'd so confidently condemned in my mind as an uncaring opportunist, stood up and walked onto the stage. He was, as it turns out, Danny's beloved pastor.

"Good call, Ed! What a scummy agent that guy is. You really do have a good feel for these things!" Louie whispered to me, then we started giggling uncontrollably. "Let us all pray," intoned the pastor solemnly, while Louie and I desperately tried to keep from laughing out loud. Somehow, this had turned into the "Chuckles the Clown" episode of *The Mary Tyler Moore Show*. (Hopefully I've learned my lesson about randomly judging strangers, though I wouldn't bet on it.)

As the memorial went on, it was filled with moments of laughter as Danny would've wanted, but also great sorrow. When his children spoke, everyone sobbed. A moving, exhausting service. After it was over, Louie and I mingled a bit with some of the family and other guests. Mayor Goodman spotted Louie and approached to say hello. "Hi, Mayor," Louie said, then gestured towards me. "Do you know comedian Ed Driscoll?" "Of course I do!" boomed the Mayor, shaking my hand. "Good to see you, Ned!" Louie and I exchanged amused glances. It's really okay to admit you don't know me, but I guess he was just trying to be polite? Or just being a politician? Regardless, it was funny. He chatted with us for a few minutes more, then said, "Anyway, I'm going to talk to some other folks. Great to see you, Louie, I love your comedy. And I'm a big fan of yours, too, Ned!", and with that, he strolled away. I looked behind me, then said to Louie, "Is there somebody named Ned around here?" And thus, "Ned" became a nickname for me from Louie for many months.

As Louie and I were walking back to our hotel on the Strip, I mentioned that I kind of wished we didn't have a show scheduled tonight. "Gonna be pretty tough to be funny after all that, right? I mean, that was a beautiful memorial, but just such a sad loss. I feel completely drained."

Louie shook his head. "No, don't worry, it will be fine. Danny would want us to do our jobs." I knew he was right, but I also knew it was going to take extra effort to perform that evening.

As it turned out, our show went incredibly well. The audience was extremely receptive, and Louie and I both had great sets. Sitting backstage afterward, I said to Louie, "Wow, wasn't that amazing? That crowd was fantastic!" Louie nodded, then said, "And do you know why I think that is? I think that our hearts were open from the memorial service today, and the audience could sense that, so they in turn, opened their hearts to us."

After a brief pause, I said, "Oh. I was gonna say, maybe they were just drunk. But I like your theory much better!"

*   *   *   *

So, what have I learned thus far, through all this — whatever "this" is? Well, most importantly, at least as far as my own personal growth is concerned, I've really come to appreciate how blessed I am. Experiencing show biz from all angles, as I've had the opportunity to do over the years, has left me with greater appreciation and understanding of not only the industry, but of myself, too.

I think the most pertinent, light-bulb moment of all came after a few years of the Hollywood grind. I was at an event, and nearby two A-list, international stars were having a conversation. Not with me, just between themselves, but I couldn't help but overhear them. (Especially when I craned my head their way just a bit.) Anyway, one was lamenting to the other about how disappointed they were about not getting a role in a new movie that was beginning production, and how they were just crushed about it. Now, this was a person who, from the outside at least, anyone would trade careers/ lives/bank accounts with in a flash. Yet they were as sad and disappointed as you'd ever hear someone express. And I thought, *wow, it never ends! No matter how "successful" you are, no matter what you've achieved, there will always be another goal, another rung on the ladder, that you'll yearn for and feel unfulfilled for not reaching.* That is, if you let the striving drive you nuts, which is easy to do. I spent a lot of time contemplating that conversation I'd overheard, and began to realize just how sinister the perils of Hollywood could be, if one wasn't constantly on guard.

Let me state clearly, I do not mean to judge or disparage the people that were having this conversation. I get it, believe me. Because generally, artists are treated pretty poorly on their way "up." Then if/when things finally go their way, they're treated ridiculously well. It can be a dizzying experience (see roller coaster analogy from introduction to this book.) It makes it hard to maintain any sense of balance. You go from hearing "You suck!" and thinking, "Yeah, I do," to hearing "You're the greatest!" and thinking, 'Yeah, I am!" — sometimes in the same day! (Or at the least, in the same week, such as my *Oscars* and *Nick Freno* ratings experience demonstrated.)

I'm often reminded of the poem *If* by Rudyard Kipling. To paraphrase, it advises that *if* you can "meet with triumph and disaster, and treat those two imposters the same," you'll find the key to a good life.

It really came home to roost for me after working on the Oscars one year. We'd had a very successful show. Billy killed it, and we were already garnering critical and popular praise, as evidenced by what I was hearing on the radio during my drive home. I was dressed in my tuxedo, tired, but happy about my own contributions to the evening, and grateful that some of my thoughts and words had actually been seen and ostensibly enjoyed by almost a billion people world-wide.

As I pulled up to my house, the trash cans were in the street from the pickup that morning. (I managed to avoid running into them as I'd done to Bob Newhart's receptacles.) So, I hopped out of the car and dragged the empty cans down my driveway and into the garage. Undoubtedly, it was an odd sight, a guy in a tux, wheeling trash bins along the asphalt. (However, the sound of empty cans on wheels sounded very similar to a drumroll, so I guess I really was dressed accordingly.) Anyway, as I was doing so, my neighbor stuck his head out the window and shouted, "Hey! Great show, Ed!" I smiled and said thanks, laughing to myself at how goofy I must look right now. And it struck me that yes, this is how life really should be lived. I'm in a tux, happy about what I'm doing, but also humbly dealing with whatever garbage-related tasks that life throws my way.

I've always been amused by the fact that if you google the term "cracking up," you're generally given two definitions:

1. To have a mental or physical breakdown.

2. To experience or cause to experience a great deal of amusement.

Pretty fine line between those two, right? Here's to all of us choosing the second definition!

ABOUT THE AUTHOR

ED DRISCOLL is an Emmy Award-winning comedian, writer and producer who has worked with some of the biggest stars in the entertainment industry including *Billy Crystal, Morgan Freeman, Joan Rivers, Michael Bublé, Justin Timberlake* and *Dennis Miller* — just to name a few! From variety shows to sitcoms to movies to live theater, Ed has been a performer, writer, and producer at the highest levels of his field for over 25 years. Ed has written for shows including *The Academy Awards* (for which he received an Emmy nomination), *Comic Relief, Stand Up To Cancer*, ESPN's *Espy Awards, Whose Line Is It Anyway*, HBO's *Dennis Miller Live* (for which he won both an Emmy and Writers Guild Award), ABC's *Sabrina The Teenage Witch*, ABC Family's *Melissa & Joey*, Comedy Central's *The Showbiz Show with David Spade*, TLC's *I Kid with Brad Garrett*, NBC's *Michael Bublé's Christmas in New York*, ABC's *The Drew Carey Show*, along with Netflix's *Ultimate Beastmaster, Still Laugh-In* and *The Final Table*. Ed has also written stage material for big acts like *Robin Williams, Bob Newhart, Howie Mandel* and *Louie Anderson*.